For Pam 23 IX 03
with best wishes
Oliver Bernard

Getting Over It

By the same author

Poetry

Country Matters (Putnam, 1961)
Poems (Samizdat, 1983)
Five Peace Poems (Five Seasons Press, 1985)
Moons and Tides, Walberswick (Southwold Press, 1989)

Translations

Rimbaud: Collected Poems (Penguin Classics, 1986)
Apollinaire: Selection (Anvil Press Poetry, 1986 –
revised bilingual edition)
Salvador Espriu: Forms and Words (Adam Biro, 1990)
The Finger Points at the Moon (Inscriptions) (Tuba Press, 1990)

Oliver Bernard

Getting Over It

An Autobiography

Peter Owen • *London*

PETER OWEN PUBLISHERS
73 Kenway Road London SW5 0RE
Peter Owen books are distributed in the USA by
Dufour Editions Inc. Chester Springs PA 19425–0449

First published in Great Britain 1992

ISBN 0–7206–0865–1

A catalogue record for this book is available
from the British Library

Printed and made in Great Britain by Braithwaite and Son Wolverhampton

For Joe and Emma and Kate
and George

Foreword

My friend Sr. Elizabeth says that *Getting Over It* is lopsided. She says it's like a confession in the confessional, and observes that that can hardly represent a complete person. 'There's a lot more to me,' she says, 'than what I say (however factual) in a confession!' And again: 'Where's your kindness and compassion for the child you were? You carry that child within you.'

I answer that it was most urgent for me to spit out and try to make sense of a great deal in my past that I couldn't digest. If I could do that, I might be able to begin to consider more pleasant questions: How did I survive? Why did I try to write verse? How can I say that I'm grateful for the life I've had and still have? Why don't I feel regret but gladness in spite of all that's happened? I can't myself wipe out blots and warts and nastiness, yet nor can I ignore the innocence which still survives.

It does survive: it doesn't just stay behind, walking across a plank bridge on a fine morning in faded shorts, aged seven. It's here and now: it has placed a whole row of reminders on the mantelshelf above the stove.

What's on the mantelshelf between the speakers, apart from eight boxes of matches in a broken packet next to the left-hand speaker? Images, postcards, poems. Messages from people I love, reminders of their affection. No bills, but the variety is greater than that in a garden. Images: a cardboard cut-out of Mr Spock from *Star Trek*; a Persian illustration of turtle-doves, a Venetian mosaic of the creation; a Bonnard bath-tub with a lady in it; another mosaic, of a stork with a snake; an Eric Gill wood engraving, *Eve, 1926* – a year younger than I, and resembling the person who sent it; a flashlight Christmas photograph of the only three adults I know who are children – I am their father; an envelope with letters in it from the Thought Factory; a postcard picture of Eleanor Marx in Ireland; a crucifix in Durham; a Van Gogh of Mme Roulin; Hercules and Antaeus on a Greek bowl with a message on the back from the *Académie de la Bière: On boit/ avec toi/sans toi*, signed *Andrée, Lucien*.

Behind the cards, more cards. A pink one to remind me that I'm Lily's godfather; invitations; a birthday card; pictures of Baudelaire, St Dunstan; even an original tiny engraving of *lovers* by my niece Lisa; a photograph of Tolstoy on a garden bench, one of Lautrec in drag. I put them all up there with the matches. They light fires too.

Truthfully, there *was* butter on my bread. There still is. It will have to be the subject of a different confession. I could even start work on it now; in fact I could probably only now begin it.

Oliver Bernard

Part One

1

Even now I hardly know whether I hated having a foreign name at school more, or less, than I hated being actually English. Not even British but English, with vestigial roots in the Home Counties and two unreconciled ancestries: a theatrical and vaguely aristocratic paternal grandfather and actress grandmother to whom my father never referred in conversation, and gave short shrift in his only published autobiographical work,* and maternal grandparents of great sweetness who lived in restricted circumstances at Norman's Bay, near Pevensey (he was a retired master butcher), about whom my mother was rather sensitive because she was snobbish.

* *Cock Sparrow* by Oliver P. Bernard (Jonathan Cape, 1936).

My parents met in the theatre in the early twenties, possibly at the Coliseum during a revival of Oscar Asche's *Chu Chin Chow*, in which my mother performed as an actress-singer and my father was the designer. They were both small physically, both extremely energetic, both strikingly handsome. In view of the rather short space of time between their marriage and the birth of my sister, and my mother's antipathy towards her, I do not think their marriage was planned or perhaps originally intended. They didn't, in the thirties' phrase, 'get on' – I can remember their fighting physically but not being more than politely affectionate. They are now, both of them, ashes scattered in the vicinity of the Golders Green Crematorium.

Life and death are not such tidy matters, though. I don't know what equipment they had at Golders Green in 1939 for dealing with fume – the finest dust of all – and it may be that my father's dust is microscopically present in very far-off places. I say my father's rather than my mother's because it is he whom I feel I have lost.

It is 1939, spring, it must be the Easter holidays. I am sitting on the floor near the fireplace in the drawing-room of a forbiddingly modern house in Dilke Street, Chelsea, near the Embankment. The house has a black bathroom, with the lavatory, bath and bidet in aquamarine. My bedroom has black walls, a pale-blue ceiling, and dark-red carpet on the floor. The drawing-room fireplace is brick, but there is an electric fire on in front of it. I am lighting old cigarette-ends of my father's – he has recently taken to smoking Player's Mild which have red instead of blue lettering on the paper – on the element of the electric fire, and sniffing the tobacco smell. I don't know where he is. I am thirteen and a half.

This is in between roller-skating on the smooth tarmac of the narrow street and the bumpy limestone flags of the Embankment pavement. At least there are no leaves from the plane trees.

Sometimes we are encouraged to go to the museums. It's an easy walk up to the King's Road, past the Chelsea Palace – 'Wednesday Night Is Carnival Night' – up Sydney Street, across the Brompton Road to South Kensington Station. There's a strange passageway under the road which brings you out at the Natural History Museum or near it. You might be coming out in the Zoo, just as coming to the top of a hill in Sussex or Hampshire you expect to see the sea. This anticipation is not, at any rate, about the Geological Survey, next to the Science Museum, which is more like an American bank than a proper museum. You can hardly 'work' anything there; perhaps just switch on a light sometimes.

Evenings at Dilke Street. It's a slightly creepy house with all that black gloss paint upstairs, but the kitchen is bright, and there are the King's Cinema and the enormous Gaumont this way and that along King's Road. The pavements have coal-hole covers of infinite variety, with names of foundries on them and so-and-so's patent. There are splendid fish shops and fruit shops which seem to stay open quite late. There seem to be artists about – my mother is amused by my younger brother Bruce's interest in beards – as well as what I hope are models, whose shoes are not good but whose legs gleam in the dusk, whose eyes are bright though their hair may be wild. They are all mystery and provocation for me, and I imagine them speaking not Cockney but foreign and low-voiced, velvet-tongued and never shrill. I am their equal in languorousness but not alas in appearance. I look not only very young but also miserable, sulky, solemn. When I smile I look stupid and even younger.

Life is pretty tense, though we sometimes laugh together. Where is my sister Sally? She is at some finishing school in Gstaad, Switzerland, where they speak German of a sort that I despise on first hearing and resist understanding. But because she is away, I suppose, my mother is having more fun being a mother, with her boys. She and the boys visit the Bar-B-Q, very modern, in King's Road, near the Gaumont, and we have our first hamburgers. We sit in a booth, and the table-cloth is red-and-white check: American.

Last time I went to the Bar-B-Q was in the fifties. Quentin Crisp was sitting at a table. I asked him how he was, noticing his hair was now mauve instead of green.

'Well, I've decided that I'm no longer Gay. I've decided to be Great.'

But in April 1939 my father is taken ill. An ulcer, which is 'perforated'. I am – we are – sent to the country, to people we don't know, on the South Downs. They keep chickens, at any rate there are large numbers of chickens close to the house in a big run, transformed by their feet into fascinating hummocks and hollows of pure mud. It's still April, stormy, bright. We slide down steep grass slopes on tin trays. Where is Daddy? Why can't we see him?

I never see him. He is ill, he is in pain, he is dying, he is dead. His funeral, what there is of it, takes place at the crematorium. His ashes, my mother says, have been 'scattered', which is what he asked to be done. I am not clear how things happen; it is all hearsay, and edited hearsay. Imagination hasn't enough to work on. I wanted to see him before he died. I wanted to see him dead. I wanted, all else failing, to see his grave. There is no such place anywhere in the world. My father is abolished. I can't, even now, think of another word.

2

The front stairs at Pachesham Lodge, Oxshott, Surrey, were well lit and open, round a square well. On the wall without a window, more than half-way up, was a framed notice in black Rockwell or a similar typeface on yellowing white: *In case that the Germans shell Poperinghe, we are obliged to go away.*

More obviously funny – I didn't learn till recently that Poperinghe was always being shelled – was a coloured cartoon showing a demented trooper in nineteenth-century French uniform running at full stretch towards the onlooker, rifle and long fixed bayonet in one hand, the other simply grasping air, mouth wide open, both feet off the ground, a storm of shells and shrapnel bursts and smoke behind him. Underneath, it said: VIVE L'EMPEREUR! And underneath that, in modern handwriting: *If only it were like that now*!

My mother called downstairs: 'Oliver!' The musicality of her call depressed me; it seemed overdone. But this time, for once, my father was in the house. I received the ambiguity head-on. I wanted to be neither her husband nor, much less so, her son.

I forget what she wanted on that occasion, but I know too well how it would have gone. Either she was going to make a suggestion for my benefit, or she would be reminding me of something I ought to be doing, or have done. I find it sickening that it would have made little difference. I'd be saying to myself: Oh lord, I suppose I've got to be nice and polite and grateful-sounding about this; or else: What a bother. The black fury of the last expression I remember distinctly because I once walked across the garden below the house on parched grass by shrubs and bushes saying 'What a bother' twenty or thirty times, head down, hating even the grass on which I'd slept in a tent for the first time the day before, and been happy.

Oxshott was where we had our last house in the country. It wasn't the most remotely situated or rural of residences, but because it was the last, and because we actually stayed there for at least two years, I remember it with some affection. There was a tennis-court and a long rockery down which water ran into and out of several ponds, ending in a small thicket of bamboos. Near the bamboos there was a large skull covered with moss, whose teeth I was always trying to loosen. I told everyone it was the skull of a rhinoceros, but it may have been some other animal. The bottom pond was the biggest and contained several frogs and newts, creatures I loved for their extraordinary beauty and wetness and agility, the gold of their eyes and the subtle variety of their skin colouring. Some of the newts I saw as dragons, giving them exaggerated scale, as I was willing to do for all sorts of creatures as well as for my model railway. I suppose this was an effort of imagination whose purpose was to surround myself with a world that was secret, beautiful and within my control or at least observation. Looking up from a flower or a blade of grass or the faintly ribbed sides of an acorn just taken from its cup, the fresh cavity only now exposed to light, I would be most unwillingly recalled to a world in which adults loomed absurdly important, and in which I was immature, and more often wrong than right.

Certain terrors, however, are also attached to Pachesham Lodge. It was in the kitchen that I saw my father transformed with anger, almost throttling my mother one evening – we were without servants at that point – because of some disagreement or indecision about which cinema we were all going to. It was in the garden there that I put into words the thought that it would be better if both my parents were dead. And at the top of the servants' staircase, leading to the main first-floor passage, I saw in a nightmare my mother's face as a mask of fear: she was being dragged by some unseen force towards the stairhead, her mouth open, but with no sound coming from it; her throat constricted with terror. I had this dream several times.

I sit typing this alone in a small house in Norfolk. Eleven o'clock on Sunday night. No traffic. No moon. A bit of black moist wind. Alone now, alone then. It would be politer perhaps to say we were four children. More cheerful too. But 'we' is a pronoun I can't use very often. We were different, and treated differently; we were separated according to age and sex; we were more often than not at different schools. My sister Sally was immensely my superior in terms of sophistication, fashion consciousness, social competence. She was and is my senior by just a year and one week. My brother Bruce was innocent compared with me, though he could play the violin with marvellous accuracy and tone. Jeffrey was what state education calls an Infant: my sister could control him with cunning, Bruce could push him into the pond, and I could stand on the brink of it anxiously encouraging him to make his weedy way to the rim and help him out of it (like the patron in Johnson's letter to Lord Chesterfield) without actually getting wet myself. To my shame, then and now.

Ten or fifteen years later, coming back from Canada, I was to have a few years of pretty close friendship with Bruce, almost as if we were meeting for the first time as brothers. But I still remember with gratefulness what Nina Hamnett said to me in the old Club des Caves de France one afternoon. It was a long and dimly lit room with an equally long bar in Dean Street, near the Colony. There were rather awful paintings on the wall opposite the bar which was presided over by Primo Carnera's brother Secondo, a grave and charming man of great size in whose hand a pint looked like a half-pint. I walked in out of the sunshine and Nina, sitting at the far end of the bar with her money in a tobacco-tin in front of her, turned and raised her eyebrows.

'Hello, Oliver! How are you?'

'I'm very well, thank you, Nina. How are you?'

'Oh, all right. How's your bloody family?'

Nowadays I should probably have leaned over and kissed her vestigial eyebrow or her wrinkled cheek. As it was, I said: 'That is a very understanding remark. Have a drink, Nina.'

I was surprised and even more pleased when she said: 'No. I'm going to buy *you* a drink. What are you having?' and reached for the tin.

Nina Hamnett buying me a drink! This was as unlikely as the time when Jeffrey, on the run I think from the army, took a white shirt out of a holdall in Wilby Mews and showed me the neckband with a peculiar grin. PAUL POTTS, it said. Soho at that time was full of people whose shirts and books had been stolen by Paul; in fact he was famous for it. But I'd never imagined anyone stealing anything from him.

3

My 'bloody family', nevertheless, evoked and confirmed feelings about them which reached back a long way. Squabbles at mealtimes, my mother's overriding voice, my sister's wail: 'It's always the boys! The boys this, the boys that!' I loathed going out as a family, my brothers' cheerfulness, my sister's misery, my mother's discipline. Only going to the Ninth Church of Christ Scientist *en bloc* kindled a spark of solidarity. Richly dressed American ladies with bosoms would bend to kiss us – my mother was the soloist – and we would all explode later in furious giggles. Sally even produced an amazing piece of subversiveness: she would stare solemnly at you and say 'Substance Matters'. This was a way of snapping shut the telescope of Mary Baker Eddy's 'Scientific Statement of Being', which I suppose was a kind of creed. Sally had good cause. She had been desperately ill at about nine when a woman guest at our house decided to ignore my mother's principles and call a doctor. I met this woman years later in Thetford: she said Sally might otherwise have died. At least that's what she said the doctor had said. Walking down Marsham Street from the 88 bus-stop in Great Smith Street, we had to pass the Salvation Army hostel, around which there were usually several poor, ill-looking men begging or just standing about with red-rimmed eyes and grey faces. You didn't have to be a young Karl Marx – or St Martin – to see the appalling contrast between that squalid hopelessness and the furs and jewels and conservative tailoring among the white marble and the water-coolers of Ninth Church. Come to think of it, the bus-stop was a stone's throw from Dean's Yard and my last school, two or three years away then. Before that, there was to be the South of France.

There is a photograph of the family, or most of it, on the terrace of a house called Villa del Sol, Roquebrune, between Monte Carlo and Menton. It is July or August 1939. My sister is in Switzerland again. I presume that the camera is being held by the housekeeper or possibly a friend of my mother's. We are revealed in our attitudes quite cruelly as it seems to me. On the left Bruce is looking confident. He has the very doubtful privilege of being my mother's favourite son. My mother looks towards him, fairly relaxed. She has just managed – a sort of triumph – to get through the business of my father's death and funeral, and our dispersal among various friends, and to organize this most extraordinary of holidays. Jeffrey, on her left, looks dependent and not too happy. I am on the extreme right, looking at the sea and probably wishing myself that far away. [This photograph is reproduced on the jacket. *Ed.*]

After our short stay on the South Downs during my father's illness and death, we were all sent to different places. I think none of us returned to school for the summer term. I landed up near Croydon with a Mrs Ferris, her small child and – at weekends – her short-haired, pink husband. She was tallish and willowy with dark hair and slightly protruding front teeth. She left me quite free most of the time to come and go.

I smoked cigarettes on the heath near the house and even visited a café on the edge of the golf-course during my long, solitary mooches. In the evening I'd have a bath and say goodnight to her. Sometimes I'd meet her in the upstairs corridor. I'd be wearing nothing but pyjama trousers, sometimes not even those. She'd laugh and say 'Are you starkers again?' and kiss me goodnight. Her lips were soft and inclined to be wet because of her sticking-out teeth. I liked her kiss. In fact I wished she'd do it more often. She was really quite exciting. But I didn't want to betray to her just how exciting I found her.

There was a maid in the daytime; I think she guessed. She sent me into the child's bedroom one afternoon to ask Mrs Ferris's permission to go out till tea-time. Her mistress was lying on the bed in her underclothes playing with the baby. I was surprised and extremely embarrassed. The maid smiled mischievously as I went out through the kitchen. I was quite irritated. The maid was younger and, superficially, more attractive than Mrs Ferris, but I thought her mean.

In France it was marvellously foreign and increasingly beautiful. Coffee from a trolley on the platform at Lyon in the middle of the night, and coffee and rolls and honey swinging round to our first sight of the Mediterranean. At Roquebrune, high above the corniche, there were lemon trees in the garden and lemon-scented mosquito repellent after dark. The terrace was a little faded and peeling but better for that, with encaustic tiles underfoot and an astounding view of the sea and of Cap Martin. There was a decent piano in the drawing-room, a woman who cooked and cleaned for us, and even a gardener, elusive and part-time.

Down many steps, across the main road, and then down still more steps, was the beach. Its big pebbles were often too hot to walk on. Out in the dazzling water were two rocks, off one of which I learnt to dive. Bruce and I spent a lot of time diving. He was better at it than I was. I don't remember whether Jeffrey had already begun to dislike the water. The pond at Pachesham Lodge was enough to put anyone off. But here it was so hot you couldn't feel afraid. The only hazard was the spines of sea-urchins.

The path and the steps were almost as interesting as the beach: fig trees and mimosa, and a hole in the corner of a stone wall where a snake was supposed to have its dwelling. I don't think we ever saw it. My attempt, the following year, to paint in gouache my memory of that pathway made me despair of painting at all. And the jobs I briefly held at Hawker's drawing offices in Kingston and Esher, and at an architect's office in Great Marlborough Street, did nothing to restore my confidence.

During the war the South of France, as we referred to it, sank into the irretrievable past. I didn't see the Mediterranean again till the end of my 1947 excursion to visit the Comtesse Pastrée, and by then I was ragged and penniless and bearded like an escaped prisoner of war, a displaced person by choice. One can see in the family photograph that the choice has already been made: *Fuir!* – to flee!

I was rescued from what would have been a very melancholy return journey *en famille* by Harold Alston.

4

The last prep school I went to was Belmont, the Mill Hill junior school, up on the Ridgeway overlooking St Joseph's RC College, with Hendon Aerodrome to the left in the distance, and the rest of London beyond. Harold Alston was school secretary when I was there, a dapper, sprightly, urbane and humorous young man going prematurely bald. He made the rest of the staff look rather tweedy and oafish. Even Arthur Rooker-Roberts, the headmaster and his close friend, looked somewhat callow beside him.

I don't know exactly how it came about that Harold became a friend. He certainly shared my father's amused contempt of organized games, and he certainly found my mother attractive and amusing. He liked the theatre, from Max Miller, whom he used to quote, to Oscar Wilde, ditto. In 1939 he took me to the Gielgud–Gwen Frangcon-Davies production of *The Importance of Being Earnest*. For some reason he got me the job of helping him to decorate his flat in the Masters' Hostel, in return for Spanish lessons. This probably freed me from cricket, though I also remember getting almost good at football the autumn before this. And I was taught to box (by Jack Geddes) to such good effect that I easily held my own in the Fifth Form and indeed knocked down a friend, who had been inclined to bully me, before forming some different alliance. Or perhaps it was then that I became a loner; only this time it was by choice.

Harold seemed to talk incessantly, and this must have helped me to say at least something – I had by the age of twelve and a half become uncommunicative and difficult. I cried a lot at home. At school I did it well away from other people. Harold encouraged me to paint, and to learn some Spanish. He spent all his holidays in Spain, mostly at Jaca, and was in love with 'abroad'. He played records of Lucienne Boyer, drank China tea without milk and ate Bourbon biscuits. He began to give me the occasional glass of sherry. On one occasion I had more than one, and on an empty stomach. When I reached the bathroom line-up still out of breath from running back from the hostel I smiled at the young matron on duty, thinking how nice she looked. I was rewarded by an answering smile and the observation that I was looking extremely naughty. I didn't know any Blake then but *Jerusalem*, or I should have told her about the poem beginning 'Why was Cupid a Boy. . . ?'

Perhaps my mother asked Harold to touch on the subject of sex in our conversations, perhaps not. I remember his warning me once about willing women. It made me feel rather cool towards him till he changed the subject. I didn't need warning about women, I needed reassuring – that eventually I should be done with this awful imprisonment in myself, this prison- or workhouse-like segregation from women, the whole nonsense. Harold was very much in the single-sex tradition, so he wasn't too good on the subject in spite of his civilized views on most things.

At the end of my stay at Roquebrune, Harold invited me to spend a few days in Paris with him and Glen Mansell, whom he afterwards married. This involved a magical solitary journey as far as Toulon or Marseille, where he was to join the train. Up to that point I talked to soldiers, who I guess were being mobilized, and who gave me fat Celtique cigarettes and swigs of rough *pinard* from felt-covered water-bottles. Chevaux 8/Hommes 40, said the goods wagons we passed; but at least this lot were in a comfortable train, and they seemed happy. I suppose none of us knew what 1939 would mean. It was still only August.

Glen got on to the train at Lyon. She had things of her own to do in Paris, so Harold took me out for breakfast from the hotel on the boulevard Haussmann, and to one or two very good meals. I tasted my first Picon-Grenadine and had my passport photograph taken. I seemed to have become much more juvenile and respectable within a few weeks.

Waiting, far from impatiently, for my mother and brothers to catch up with us, I stayed at Belmont, which was empty, savoured the memory of the young matron, and learnt to play squash. I was still there on Sunday morning, 3 September, and eating a large Victoria plum in the kitchen garden when the air-raid sirens sounded somewhere down the Ridgeway.

5

If Harold Alston was the only schoolmaster – he began teaching the year after I left Belmont – who seemed to me actually ahead of my own wishes for escape from childhood, there had been another teacher at a previous school who had been alongside, as a gentle friend. This was Norman Wormleighton. The school was Bunce Court.

I wish I knew more about the history of Bunce Court. It was absolutely unique, not just among my schools but in Britain. How my father got to know about it, and why we were removed from it, were questions I found equally unanswerable. The school had arrived *en bloc* from Germany, somewhere near Mannheim, at the beginning of the Hitler period. When we got there in 1935 there were seven or eight British pupils and about 120 German Jewish boys and girls. The staff was more heavily British, since teaching was conducted, except for German language and literature, in English. It had been known as the Neue Herrlingen Schule.

The headmistress was Dr Anna Essinger. I suspect she was a Quaker, not a religious Jew. She was known as Tante Anna – Aunt Anna. Other senior members of staff were Tante Paula and Frau Kahn. I'm not sure that either of these women taught at school. I think they were in charge of the food and accommodation. But they were not different in status from any teacher. Of the teaching staff I remember Mr Brind (science) and Mr Prag, known as 'Praha', who taught maths. Norman taught English. He had a pretty young wife called Susan. I don't think she taught there. Hans Meyer had us up in the morning doing a sort of physical jerks before breakfast. Hannah Goldschmidt, 'Hago', taught German. What did 'Hutschnur' do?

At first it was simply strange and slightly frightening, though I still remember the sweetness of an older girl who showed us where to sleep on our first night. Like all new places it seemed very big, and like all new schools rather threatening. Somehow all that changed and was forgotten. Sally slept in the girls' bit, Bruce was down the road in what was called the Little House, and I stayed somewhere in the middle of the main house, with Ulli Borchardt and Gabriel Adler and Fred Abrahams and everyone. We had to wash up, and polish floors with heavy blocks, and make toast on Saturdays, and get hold of the language. *Blöder Gans*, for instance, could be said quite openly, whereas *Angeschissenes Bettgestell* could not.

The presence of girls in class-rooms and on bicycle rides and bonfire nights and at table was strange and interesting. Women teachers were not absolutely unknown; but they were a nice change and not at all spinsterish. 'Hutschnur' was graceful, 'Hago' was as creamily beautiful as fudge.

I had a stand-up fight with Fred Abrahams, and was soothed by Betty MacPherson, whom I loved. I was nine. She had straight bobbed hair and slightly protruding, greenish-blue eyes. I'd never met anyone kinder or more serious. She told me about tartans, and I let her have first go on my new bicycle on a freezing December morning in 1935. I'm afraid this was about the extent of our relationship. She was older than I, and I must have been of very much less interest to her than she was to me. It wasn't painful, though. She went on being kind and friendly. I found things to do.

Bunce Court doesn't sound very magical, the way I'm describing it. The wonderful thing about it was the way it allowed things to happen. Not only was no one ever physically assaulted there by a member of staff in the name of discipline, but no one was afraid of anyone. It was a community. We dug our own swimming-pool; we went on a huge bike ride and camped somewhere near Rye. When a tall bonfire was beginning to die down, teachers ran and jumped across the wide bed of red-hot embers with a small boy between them. There was a gramophone club that anyone could go to. There were plays in an open-air theatre dug out like a small Greek one, with cypresses at the back of the platform. We went for enormous walks far into the dusk, and sang *Lauf, jäger, lauf.*

6

The Wormleightons were kind people. Norman loomed large, a sort of Anglo-Saxon hero, even a king: ring-giver, leader, host. He was tall, fair, bearded and benign. He let me read the Fool to his Lear in the class-room standing on its own among the ash saplings, heated by a Tortoise stove whose pipe stuck out of the corrugated-iron roof. 'Not "war-son" but "horse-un", Olly,' he politely corrected me. 'Prithee, nuncle, be contented; 'tis a naughty night to swim in.' I could always go and ask him things. I seemed to amuse him, and he could smile me out of some anxieties. But being sent to boarding-school never became ordinary or acceptable, and was no relief from the stormy emotional weather at home.

It was Norman who took us for the long ride to camp, and Norman who consoled me when I dropped a precious packet of five Player's Weights in a wet ditch. He ran the gramophone club; he possessed an EMI machine with a great papier-mâché horn, and which used cane needles. But it was Praha the mathematician, who lived in the main house (Norman and Susan had a cottage half-way to Warren Street from the school), who found me wandering about unable to sleep, and took me for a long walk that frosty night and pointed out the stars and constellations without referring to the strangeness of the hour or to whatever it was that was biting me. There was plenty for a while: an attempt was made to make me right-handed; I wet the bed, including once a pair of Ulli Borchardt's pyjamas with glass buttons. 'Hutschnur' undertook to get me up late to have a piss, but it took a long time to solve the problem. I think they gave up the right-handed campaign after a term.

I must have told Praha about my visits to the woods of Otterden

Park, where a gamekeeper, after scolding me (I could have shot you, he said), agreed to let me come on his rounds with him, and I became acquainted with the smell of gunpowder and the flurry of the shot rabbit. At first I had gone into the woods because they were magic, and found jays' feathers, wild strawberries, all kinds of moss, beechmast, little skulls. Praha said I should bring some back, and even wrote a notice for my exhibit: OPEN YOUR EYES. Unfortunately the first container I begged had contained kippers, so there were wags who commented, with the German accent I came to like: 'And close your nose!'

Guessing about Bunce Court now, where at ten years old I learnt the names of all the Nazi leaders, and learnt to hate dictators and anti-Semitism, and could chant, in 1935, in the Garden of England:

Parade marsch! Parade marsch!
Hitler hat ein loch in arsch!

it must have been my father's idea. He is the only professional, ex-army Englishman I've ever heard of who returned from America saying that the only people who were really humane or kind there when he was in difficulties were Jews. He probably thought it a good idea for us to learn German, too. As for our leaving, which still seems to me a very unlucky event, it may be that he was prevailed upon by my mother, who was slightly (that is to say, quite sufficiently) anti-Semitic, and expressed more pride in our going to 'the Mill Hill junior school' than I ever heard my father utter. 'Organized loafing' was what he called cricket. But this may be unjust to my mother. Bruce says he was very homesick at Bunce Court because the language (outside lessons) was German. It was something like being abroad. This may have decided the change of school. I didn't mind the German myself, though.

7

These memories are not so much confused as disordered. My eldest son Joe says so, my (Carmelite) Sister E says so. My life, though I lived it pretty intensely, was for a very long time out of my control. Our frequent moves from house to house and from London to the country and back, and mine from school to school, were devastating upheavals, and Sister E is probably right when she guesses that even my parents did not know why things happened in the particular time sequence – I avoid calling it 'order' – in which they did happen. Together or separated, they were not happy people. Eight o'clock Mass at Quidenham this morning was celebrated with a body in the nuns' choir, coffined and flanked by tall candles. It was Sr. Veronica, dead at eighty-nine, and smilingly remembered. Praying briefly for my parents at the appropriate point in the bidding prayers, I thought: *They were unhappy*. It didn't occur to me at that moment that they might have been 'right' or 'wrong'.

During August 1939, as John Field's history of the school says, 'Westminster was packed up and moved to Sussex. . . . Houses were rented in Shoreham . . . to take the overflow of boys whom Lancing and Hurstpierpoint could not house.'

Term began on 20 September. I don't know from which house or flat I travelled to Lancing and then to Shoreham. I think it may have been Mrs Hince's house in Boundary Road, Swiss Cottage. Hamish Wilson, stage designer and crony of my mother's, and brother of the very small actor Ian, made up a sort of tongue-twister about Mrs Hince: 'Mrs Hince has six sisters all spinsters.' Her house was very comfortably furnished, and contained – besides gin and whisky – joss-sticks, and a strange brown powder that it took me some time to identify as snuff. I remember trying to smoke it, which gave me trouble with my mouth and saliva. Among the books in the drawing-room was Boccaccio's *Decameron*, which included the bawdy story about Rustico and Alibech. The curtained drawing-room and its Victorian furnishings, the very binding of the two-volume Victorian edition, seemed to suggest that it was not so much cheerfully bawdy as dangerously wicked. A visit to the drawing-room to consult the book was thus a whole expedition into sinfulness which I carried out like a spy, my heart in my mouth. I needed someone to tell me what – between pleasure at its frankness and the threat of an avalanche of punishment – I already guessed: it's a *joke*, Oliver. Why were adults so afraid of smiling? The appalling pressure can be taken off in seconds – I was about to say, the ghost can be easily laid.

I don't know so much about first terms at schools. I found Westminster, even evacuated to Lancing – 'Top hats should not be brought' –

frighteningly superior with its special jargon, its rules written and otherwise, and its dizzying hierarchies. I'm grateful only that I could, like Anthony Wedgwood Benn (as he then was, a year my senior), opt for Scouts instead of the OTC. And that my rather awed respect for King's Scholars in academic gowns like Michael Hamburger was actually part of the Westminster ethos. I don't, I'm afraid, ever get tired of telling people how I overheard two fourteen-year-olds discussing an older boy, and how one of them said: 'He's frightfully *learned*, you know.' 'Swot' was not an expression much used at Westminster, though it may have been at Greyfriars. And despite my awful handwriting I have at least one cheerful memory of lesson times: that of the clear and acerbic voice of a young Latin master responding to my growing habit of jumping up and down at my desk, hand raised to give the answer to a translation question, shrieking 'Sir! Sir!' – 'Sit DOWN, Bernard!'

8

I met and talked and drank with at least one of my contemporaries at Westminster in the York Minster, the French pub (now so named) in Soho, in the fifties – John Raymond, the journalist and critic. Despite his pomposity and his frequent allusions to slap-up meals past, present and to come, he was impossible to dislike. He had I think acquired a sort of armour of blustering 'forthrightness' – which I put in quotes, since we all choose exactly what to be forthright about – which, together with his clear, high-pitched, upper-class schoolboy's voice, made him both amusing and engaging. As a junior I recall his being sensitive and quiet, and I think he went in terror of being what was called 'had' by some piratical homosexual older boy. I remember we were both rather frightened and fascinated by Freddy Hurdis-Jones, to whom I used to refer as the 'egregious' Freddy, but whom I have long since regarded as the amazingly courageous Freddy.

At Mardon Hall, Exeter University, where we were again evacuated from Lancing, there was a political debate on party lines at which a somewhat naïve-looking and painfully honest 'Labour' speaker was 'Wedgwood Benn'. He began, very nervous, by addressing us as 'Ladies and Gentlemen'. There being no ladies present, Freddy got up from his chair – we were all wearing sports jackets and flannels – and, raising the skirts of his chocolate-coloured jacket, said, in his rather deep and beautiful voice: 'I'm Glad you've Discovered my Sex.' We were so amused and so appalled that I don't honestly remember what happened. Perhaps nothing. Tony Benn continued; he too was not without courage.

My only close friend at Westminster was Michael Nesbitt. We met early in our first term. We had both lost our fathers.

17 June 91

> Dear Ms Nesbitt,
>
> Please excuse this note if I turn out to be mistaken in my feeling that you may perhaps be related to Michael Nesbitt [Tom Nesbitt's son], who was my friend in 1939 and 1940 at Westminster School. . . . We lost touch after that, and at the same time I ran away from home, so that it would have been difficult in any case to remain in touch. . . .

Michael's father had been an actor and his chief interest was architecture. Mine had been an architect – his entrance to the Strand Palace Hotel is, at the time of writing, at the V & A waiting to be reassembled and exhibited – and before that had worked in the theatre. My mother was also a performer. His mother now ran the Sloane Bridge Club in Hans Road, behind Harrods, though she had also appeared on the stage – less prominently than his famous aunt Kathleen, whom I saw in *Outward Bound* at the 'Q' Theatre towards the end of her career. The Sloane Bridge Club clientele was stagy, too. I once helped extinguish an incendiary bomb on the pavement outside. Michael amused me with imitations of his mother's club members. There was one old drunk who used to shout: 'My Gud, they've forgutten those cucktails!' And there was an ex-actress who used to climb the staircase from Hans Road and declaim in a descending arpeggio: 'My – dear – I'm – *dead*!'

Michael's elder sister Prue was tall and beautiful. My own sister was much amused by Michael, who was very tall for his age, partly because he had had something like a tubercular knee-joint that had involved surgery. He had spent a long time in bed, where he had apparently grown a lot, and his leg was stiffened; he wore a contraption of metal and leather, a brace. This gave him a rather jaunty yet ponderous gait and enabled him to use a cane. He and I spent considerable time together at school and in the holidays admiring Georgian houses and fantasizing about the late eighteenth century. We used to like walking up St James's past White's and Boodle's and dropping in at Fribourg and Treyer's to buy Balkan Sobranie cigarettes. Jermyn Street and the 'Burlers Arkers' saw us not infrequently. We gambled in our heads more than womanized, though I think I was less interested in gambling than he. Affairs of honour ran in his mind, and he read a lot of Jeffrey Farnol, whom I couldn't get on with. I preferred the prose poetry of Poe's *Tales* and the excitement of Sherlock Holmes's problems.

Michael told me all about Beau Brummell and his quarrel with the Prince Regent: 'Alvanley! Who's your fat friend?' This was followed by Brummell's death in destitution and madness in France, pretending that he was a major-domo announcing the arrival of guests, banging a long ceremonial stick on the floor:

(Bang, bang, bang.) His Royal Highness the Prince Regent!

Pause.

(Bang, bang, bang.) George Bryan Brummell!

At which point he would 'fall down in a fit, frothing at the mouth'.

This got telescoped, in the manner of my brother Jeffrey's early film-scripts, into 'George Bryan Brummell, froth-pom'.

Jeffrey began, as many people must do, by amusing his family. He still does that, of course. But I was reminded of his early essays the other day, watching my black-and-white portable TV which comes into its own when revived British war time films are shown in the afternoon. The film I was watching was about the heroic few of the RAF. Suddenly I saw the epitome of this film itself in a couple of lines of dialogue, and it reminded me of Jeffrey's very short film about the wartime navy:

Officer on bridge, stares through binoculars at horizon.

RATING (*mounts ladder, faces officer, salutes*): Excuse me, sir, torpedoes fore and aft. We're sinking fast.

OFFICER (*lowers binoculars with infinite weariness but does not cease to gaze at horizon, face lined and tanned, jaw bulldog, etc. Very slowly, as if complaining of adverse cricket weather*): Damn this *bloody* war.

Jeff had another film about a hospital, with a surgeon saying to a patient completely swathed in bandages: 'Medical science has made tremendous advances in the last few years, but in the final analysis, *it's up to you*.'

9

To my surprise and dismay, in 1940 Michael ceased abruptly to have anything to do with me. This is what happened. A woman friend of his family's, an attractive French-speaking widow (merry enough, and kind too), who had cigarettes made for her with her initials on them, invited us to a party at the height of the Battle of Britain. I don't remember much about the party, but towards the end of it the air-raid sirens sounded and I telephoned my mother in Lansdowne Walk to say that I had been told I could stay the night in South Kensington rather than try to travel back to Holland Park, thus avoiding showers of shrapnel or shell fragments walking to and from underground stations. I could hear her anxiety, I could almost see her beyond the bottle glass of the front door (though that would have been blacked out), standing at the telephone looking dark and angry.

The guests, including Michael, left. The spare room was small but it had a large elegant wardrobe with a mirror inside the door. I slipped out of a sort of early T-shirt with a Jermyn Street label that had belonged to my father and got into bed. My hostess came in to say goodnight. She was dressed for bed herself. She stayed with me for quite a long while and managed me very pleasantly and skilfully. She smelt of whisky and said over and over again: 'It's natural, darling, it's natural, naatchurrrl. . . .'

It was in fact so natural to me that in the morning, at some frightfully early hour for adults with hangovers, I went to her room and said words to the effect that I wanted to do it again. She was very cross and because of this looked much less attractive than she had a few hours earlier. She told me in no uncertain terms to *go away*.

Her annoyance with me was not so very much unlike my mother's anger. I became angry myself. I stole her cigarette-case before leaving.

It was the theft I felt bad about, sitting at South Kensington station waiting for a train. I could almost see her flat from where I sat, down on the platform. But about being a young man of fourteen and a half I felt very good indeed. I whistled, when I could stop smiling. But it was so painful, when I told Michael, to see his reaction (Was it his leg? His mother's friend? Incest? Unchastity?), that I cannot recall our conversation. I really had no other friend of my age.

Sitting in Devon this cold wet June, trying to remember, it occurs to me that it is intensity and not duration that I know about. Life at school – my whole boyhood – seemed at the time, and therefore still seems, to have lasted far longer than it did. I'm more than three times the age I was when I got my first rejection slip from *Men Only* for a short story while I was serving out my time in the RAF in 1946; and more than four times the age at which I ran away from home; yet my few terms at Westminster seemed like years and years; my jobs and experiences of 1941 seem a whole age long. And now, puzzling over my willed and welcome seduction of 1940, and Michael Nesbitt's reaction to it, it occurs to me that I was a thief, and that Michael must have known it.

10

A great many good things and some extraordinary ones happened while I was at Westminster. I mean apart from the depressing news of Dunkirk, and the awful cabbage smell of Lancing refectory. Michael and I skipped off to Brighton and drank beer in the Cricketers. We discussed the merits of various exotic cigarettes – sold loose, about twenty-four to the ounce – with a grave and charming Brighton tobacconist, whose reply to my rather phonily elegant and worldly inquiry, 'These look quite interesting. Who actually makes them?' almost bereft us of speech: 'Te-o-fani, sir. A good house, I believe.' Perhaps he twigged how young we were. He certainly gave a splendid performance.

I was told, to my joy, that I could, if I preferred to do so, row instead of playing football or cricket. So I spent many weeks alone in a skiff on the River Adur, learning to balance it with my oars and eventually astonishing myself if no one else with my speed over the mushroom-coloured water.

A young friend of my father's came and took me out to tea a few times. I'm afraid I had to fend him off a bit; but he was really very kind and intelligent. He sent me a Temple *Shakespeare's Sonnets*, a beautiful little scarlet book, almost square, which burst on me like a sudden shower while the sun is still blazing.

O, how I faint when I of you do write.

One of our outings on a Saturday afternoon was to Chanctonbury Ring, high up on the Downs, the most beautiful congregation of beech trees I've ever seen. And there was a long walk in the Downs that the Scouts did, through landscape which I saw again years later in Blake's

The lost Traveller's Dream under the Hill.

One evening on the fine gravel at Lancing after prep, supercooled rain fell and immediately turned to black ice. Another night, the aurora borealis marched down the sky, also rather Blakean. Mr Carleton, who taught history, cheerfully greeted one with Cockney-derived urbanity: 'Mwotcha!' His later corporal punitiveness had not yet manifested itself.

But my career at Westminster ended badly indeed. I still feel uncertain about the *post hoc* and *propter hoc* of it. At Shoreham, in our billets, I stole a ten-shilling note which I found lying on a chest of drawers. After a great deal of talk about it in my house, and much fruitless investigation, I felt so bad about it that, never having spent it but only changed it into four half-crowns which I hid in a brick wall in a back street in Shoreham, I went and confessed to my housemaster, a man with few resources beyond conventional wisdom, vague kindness and a rather unsophisticated sense of humour. I mean, he may have had important virtues but these were not available or apparent at the time. This was in the so-called spring term of 1940. I was sent to the headmaster, J.T. Christie, and duly beaten. My score now stood at thirteen: six for eating toffee in his divinity lesson – he was the author of a book called *The Personality of St. Paul*, a buff-coloured paperback volume of which we were all given a copy, though I don't know whether or not it went on the bill – and seven for stealing.

I was deeply ashamed. My weals were treated nightly in the sick-bay. I contracted diphtheria – the only boy in the school to do so. Diphtheria seems to have been a disease that affected poor people. I thought I must have caught it from or at the place where I had hidden the half-crowns in the wall. Be that as it may, I spent several weeks in Hove Hospital, becoming acquainted with blanket baths, black stockings as part of a nurse's uniform, the drinking cup with a spout, and the bedpan. The water was redolent of chlorine. The South Downs were pale and cold. I climbed up into the water-tower and could see the water in the huge, deep and silent tank. The metal ladder actually came up through a kind of tube or hole in the tank itself. Ugly it may have been, but the sheer scale of it was wonderful. I made the journey several times during my convalescence. There was little to do in the hospital, though I may have been given some school work to do. I forget.

I was almost forgetting the entire episode when it occurred to me, six months later, that my seductress's cigarette-case must have been missed. She may even have mentioned it. *I* may even have told Michael about it. So here was a second and confirming instance: I was a thief, then. Unlike Raffles, I should add. A thief with no class at all, and no high score at Lord's. A dirty, little. . . . I wonder if it was that.

I was never quite sure whether I'd been expelled or asked to leave. Yet in the summer term of that year my bit of Westminster was at Exeter University, at Mardon Hall, and I was there too. I remember the sort of hole under the cliff near the railway station. I even remember Donald Swann and another senior boy in some rather pleasant and sympathetic conversation in which I couldn't, as a junior, imagine joining in, but which made me feel that it might be possible to graduate as it were into civilized life. Also I had my father's typewriter at Exeter: a red Royal shading to black at the edges. And I was reading a university library copy, pale-blue cloth bound, of Trotsky's *History of the Russian Revolution*. I even thought up some sort of manifesto. So I can't have been expelled.

11

Because Belmont had been the only school out of the six I went to that I left from the top, instead of being transferred arbitrarily to another school, I knew it in a different way from the others. I've already said that Harold Alston made the young headmaster Arthur Rooker-Roberts look a bit callow; but he was not callow, just less witty and world-weary. He loved to entertain. The reception after his wedding, which happened while I was there, in the holidays, was a most dazzling affair, I'm told. The house, Belmont, is an Adam-style building with a beautiful round staircase. The doors off it are curved and the stone stairs are keyed and self-supporting, seemingly without weight, aerial. Outside is or was a marvellous cedar tree.

Arthur and Brenda seem to me no less wonderful than the Kennedys at their zenith: beautiful people is not putting it too strongly. He had a fast car in which he took boys for rides, a Railton, and I used to have a photograph of Harold sitting at the wheel of this car, looking rakish. He had all sorts of gadgets that he loved showing people, and a wonderful electric record-player we lay on the carpet listening to on Sunday evenings, fifteen at a time. Brenda used to let me look at big Phaidon art books during these music sessions. I found her enchanting.

Brenda's mother, Mrs Clarke, was actually in charge of all domestic arrangements at Belmont, and had, besides Brenda, two sons whom I met at Ashford just before the war. I hung out of my bedroom window listening to Hugh Clarke and his friend Jack Clark who had the radio on. Hitler speaking at one of those rallies, a scream of rage. The house was outside Ashford on the side of a hill. Hugh and Jack walked me to the pub before dinner and bought me shandy. Jack explained to me what capitalism was, and showed me the first copy I'd ever seen of the *Daily Worker*.

Returning to London in Jack's car or Hugh's, I remember seeing British Union of Fascists slogans somewhere about Croydon, saying MIND BRITAIN'S BUSINESS, with the lightning-flash sign. I could not make head or tail of this. Hugh Clarke was killed flying a Spitfire in the Battle of Britain – another one of the beautiful people. But I was to see Jack Clark again.

In the last two terms I spent at Belmont, I chose to join in a mass swim before breakfast every morning in the unheated open-air swimming-pool. It was Arthur's idea, and none of us wore anything or moved at less than top speed. Sometimes we had to break the ice. We ran back to breakfast, Arthur laughing along with us. He laughed a lot, and liked playing word games with his top form. He taught us the alphabet which begins: A for orses; B for mutton; C for yourself. The bit I liked best was the juxtaposition L for leather and M for sis. After the war Bruce and I went to see him one evening and, typically, he offered us pewter tankards of beer – quart tankards.

12

By the time I left Westminster, or rather did not return to it at the end of the summer holidays, and ceased to see Michael Nesbitt, the war had moved into the phase between Dunkirk and the invasion of the USSR. The news was of ships sunk and aircraft shot down, of war in the desert and of the turning of Europe from a battlefield into a German fortress. London was full of air-raid shelters, and shrapnel on the pavements, and uniforms. The sky was sown with barrage balloons: there was one in Ladbroke Square. People became more sky conscious, and it began to matter whether a night was clear or cloudy. Rationing got a little tighter. Mr Jenkins's dairy in Portland Road became an important place. His face, lean and irritable, narrowly watched the scales. He seemed to let butter go unwillingly, and count money into the till disgusted with the smallness of the amount. He was probably having a hard time of it.

I went for a time to Davies, Laing and Dick, the tutorial establishment in Holland Park which Dom Moraes was attending when I met him in 1955, my age having exactly doubled in the meantime. I remember little about it, and only suppose that I was studying towards something like School Certificate, for which I'm pretty sure I never sat. Although there was plenty of talk about the shortage of money (the real reason I had left Westminster), I was never informed about my mother's finances. I assume that Davies, Laing and Dick was not cheap, and that Mr Rees, who visited me for lessons in maths in Lansdowne Walk, was cheaper. Why I was shipped off to stay with him and his wife I still don't know.

At Hertford Heath Mr and Mrs Rees had a tidy post-1914–18 detached house near the common. He taught at Haileybury, biology I think, and was thin, ascetic-looking, grave and polite. He had seemed so out of place in London that I felt almost protective towards him, but life in Hertford Heath was very quiet and regular. He managed to smile despite looking rather ill sometimes, and tired when he got back from school. One Saturday morning outside a teashop in Hertford he was taken ill and had to sit on the pavement. He dabbed white foam from his mouth – his lips were bluish – with a white handkerchief. I thought this might be an epileptic attack but never dared ask.

At the Reeses' I was shown surprising kindness. Mrs Rees set me tasks in English and made me read the Brontës, Jane Austen, Thomas Hardy, George Eliot. She even suggested walks I should take, and listened to what I had seen. When I had a cough she rubbed Vicks into my chest.

I was dogged by guilt and uncertainty. It seemed that my piercing sense of the beauty of things and people dragged behind it a long shadow of self-disgust: I was hopelessly mean, cowardly, self-indulgent, I decided. I actually got so worried about masturbating that I spoke to Mr Rees about it. This may sound simple enough, but it was agonizingly difficult. The only way I could do it was to say that something was worrying me and then partly allow what I had to say to be dragged out of me patiently by Mr Rees, and partly to utter words with such labour that each one seemed like a large stone that had to be lifted by brute strength. A complete sentence felt like a day's work.

His comment was interesting. When he had asked me why it seemed so dreadful, and I had answered, by now in floods of tears which I strained desperately to check, that 'it seemed such a terrible waste', he said: 'Now that is very interesting. The wastefulness of nature. Yes. Well, you see, nature *is* wasteful. All I can say is, don't worry too much about all this. Things will settle down eventually.' I was more aware of his strange aloofness and coolness at the time than of his kindness and tact, but at least he hadn't made me feel worse and was someone to be trusted. I was puzzled about the cozy liveliness of Mrs Rees and the contrast with the rather haunted manner of Mr Rees. There was an extraordinary reproduction hanging in their bedroom that seemed quite alien to everything else in the house but that must have been very personal to them both. It represented a young girl and a boy standing facing each other in a classical-looking landscape – a sentimental, bluish-green, turn-of-the-century subject, it seemed to me. They were both beautifully modelled, both naked, somewhat idealized. It was a mystery. On the landing with its brown linoleum and cream paint, or downstairs in the chintzy drawing-room (chintzy was a term of contempt in my mother's mouth), it was impossible to believe that the picture existed at all except in a dream.

There were a lot of pleasant things about Hertford. It had a marvellous little neoclassical town hall which I tried to draw. The river – I hope it was the Mimram — swirled under a bridge near the town museum, to which I became a regular visitor. I remember little of its contents. It seemed always deserted, dusty, sad. There were the usual cases of flint arrowheads and axes, labelled in a sort of depressed copperplate; some bones; some ill-lit portraits of former Hertfordshire worthies; stuffed animals and birds. It was a nice quiet place to smoke, and it pleased me to, as it were, sit on the past rather than have the past sitting on me. Out of one of the rare windows I could see the river and a pair of oast-houses. But before I visited them I put a penny into the slot of an enormous glass-fronted musical box which obliged with some rattling and grinding and the loud tune of a nineteenth-century song about rural life. It was not 'To Be a Farmer's Boy' but something about going to a fair. The round brass face of the machine agreed with the cyclic and repetitive nature of the melody, and the echoes when it stopped ran away past cobwebs and dust into the cream-painted walls already full of old, dead conversations.

I tried to draw the oast-houses, or rather malt kilns, and one afternoon I decided to see them from as close as possible. Hanging about – something I became very good at indeed – in the maltster's yard, I was invited inside on a wonderfully cold clear winter's day, and sat thrilled and comfortable at the red fire opening with a couple of oldish men. The maltster himself was kind enough, when he understood that I was 'studying' and making sketches, to show me the malt floors with their unglazed windows and explain the need for sprouting the barley before roasting it. He showed me the upper floor of the kiln, still warm, whose steel mesh was like the mesh of a paper-maker's mould which gives a ribbed watermark. There were little pockets of malted barley to taste, the colour of pale milk chocolate, and delicious in spite of the hard fibres. I walked back uphill past thorn hedges and field gates feeling I had not wasted the day.

13

Just once, at one of my schools, I read some reference to Wilhelm Stekel. I rather think it was some tract I was reading by a medical man, who linked Stekel's name absurdly with that of Krafft-Ebing, and denounced them both as evil, obscene and so forth. I did not come across a book by Stekel until the end of the seventies, forty years later, when I found in a second-hand bookshop in Norwich for 75p, a copy, fairly clean, bound in orange buckram, of *Auto-Erotism*, reprinted in 1951 by Peter Nevill (who do not bother to include the information that the book first appeared about 1920).

In my copy of *Auto-Erotism* there is a curious rubber stamp on the flyleaf: HALF-PRICE WILL BE ALLOWED IN CREDIT ON RETURN OF THIS BOOK, AGAINST OTHER BOOKS PURCHASED FROM US. The ink is so faint that I've managed to decipher the words only with a magnifying glass. This is no mystery. I remember Bob Katz, a friendly 'dirty-bookshop' person in Soho in the fifties (he was one of the very few people from Soho who attended Robert Colquhoun's funeral with me in 1962) explaining that much of his income came from the system of 'selling' books to customers and then accepting them back at half price. It was like running a really expensive lending library. He added that 'vicars like fladge books'. So Stekel's book suffered the same fate as another of my best finds, the Ezra Pound translation of Rémy de Gourmont's *Physique de l'amour – The Natural Philosophy of Love*.

I had read about the Gourmont book somewhere and inquired for it in many places in London without success. I found it eventually in Moor Street, Cambridge Circus, in a now disappeared 'dirty bookshop': it was in the window among much less edifying stuff, and I took a deep breath before entering the place. It is a delightful book, and I had not reread it for a long time when Lucian Freud appeared in one of my two Soho pubs the other day. He and another man were talking about translation. I ventured to state my conviction that the most important thing of all about a translator is that he should know his *own* language as perfectly as possible. Lucian's face lightened and he began to talk about Pound and *The Natural Philosophy of Love*. 'Ah,' said I. 'There's a book!' And we happily discussed Gourmont's description of the mating of dragonflies in chapter XIII, and how it is far more exciting than a description of anything human. He is the only other person I know who is familiar with it, though I suppose some poets know it. George Barker knew it.

But what were Stekel and Gourmont doing in dirty bookshops? And what had British education been doing for me in the thirties? 'Paying one's debt to society' is a phrase familiar to everyone. How unfamiliar the idea that society should pay its debt to children! Or is it a romantic mistake of mine to believe that children are *owed* – that they arrive in credit and remain so during their schooling? I don't say that a certain reciprocity ought not to develop before young people become adults, but to feed lies to the innocent on subjects that are of the greatest importance to them is simply wicked. What percentage of the population do you imagine were in the habit of masturbating quite cheerfully until the day they discovered that it was a 'dangerous' habit, leading to 'moodiness and depression' and eventually 'incapacitating' the person who indulged? Dr Gutheil in his 1949 foreword to Stekel's book compares Stekel with Semmelweiss, who suffered ridicule and ostracism when he revealed the way in which puerperal fever was spread in maternity hospitals. He reminds the reader that Semmelweiss later was 'rightly referred to as "the Saviour of Mothers"' and suggests that for helping 'to free the young generation from the all-pervading feeling of anxiety, the hypochondriacal anticipation, and the profound guilt feelings caused by misinformation, Stekel deserved the name "Saviour of Youth"'.

Well of course youth still needs saving; we all do, because whether we like it or not

> We are all children
> And we must all die.

Sir Isaac Newton thought of himself in old age as a boy wandering along the sea-shore, picking up a few interesting pebbles; dictators are increasingly understood by psychologists as abused children asserting some personal version of their parents' former omnipotence; even the precious medical profession includes people who so much lack confidence or competence that they will do and say almost anything rather than relinquish their title to infallibility; but I am sitting here in 1992 saying: you will know enough about what interests you when you are dead, and vice versa, so keep learning. Lucian Freud does, George Barker did. Me, I'm learning to write this book. Trying to, at any rate.

14

Charles Graham, who runs the Tuba Press and edits a poetry magazine called TUBA, amuses me by sending me postcards with quotations handwritten on the back. These usually have nothing to do with the pictures on the cards, or with the printed matter on the back. Thus what looks like a big water-colour with female figures on a river bank has a Blake proverb in Charles's clear, round hand as well as this printed information:

> THE RIVER TANG P.C. 2055 By courtesy of the City of Manchester Art Galleries.
>
> PHILIP CONNARD (1875–1958) worked as a house-painter and attended art classes in the evenings until he won a scholarship to the Royal College of Art. He also studied in Paris but returned to London to teach art while at the same time designing textiles and illustrating books in a late Pre-Raphaelite style. He was an official war artist to the Royal Navy for the years 1916–1918 and his varied career also included painting a number of murals, for buildings in New Delhi, for the liner *Queen Mary*, and for the Queen's Doll's House at Windsor.
> © The Medici Society Ltd., London. Printed in England.

I'm not sure that my father was acquainted with Philip Connard before we went to live at Richmond, next door to him. My father's war service straddles Connard's but the navy and the army spent little time actually shoulder to shoulder. True, my father had to camouflage some naval guns in the Nieuport Sector in 1917, but Connard was a war artist and not a camouflage officer or a naval gunner. I think it is more likely that they were both members of the Chelsea Arts Club.

The house we lived in for about a year, between Oxshott and Dilke Street, was in Cholmondeley Walk, on the towpath just below Richmond Bridge on the Surrey side, opposite what I now discover is called Corporation Island. From it we were often sent along the towpath with a supply of sandwiches and a thermos flask to Kew Gardens, which had a special little gate on the towpath called Isleworth Ferry Gate, and was a most magnificent pennyworth. It was a wonderful walk in any case, with a railway bridge and a road bridge to go under, and Richmond

Lock to look at, and Syon Park to wander about, beyond the rushes on the Middlesex side, and pleasure-boats going up and down, and big trees at the edge of the Old Deer Park.

The towpath was sometimes flooded, which was very pleasing. My father, however, built a sort of dam between the gate and the front door. It would be ironic if this set of brick steps has survived while his extraordinary mural decorations for the Oxford Corner House in various colours of marble have disappeared. There was in any case something piquant about an architect laying bricks. It put him in a good mood, and reminded me of a time at Oxshott when he had said to me: 'Let's have a look at your hands.' I had shown him them, without speaking. My hands were like his – something I was very glad about: squarish, large-palmed, with short fingers. 'Yes,' he said, looking amused. 'You'll be a navvy.'

The Richmond house was the property of Major Longden, who certainly had been an army colleague; a 'buffer', I suppose one could call him, harmless, rather gentle. Bruce and I discovered an old Lee-Enfield rifle in the attic with which we used to 'shoot' people in Friar's Lane, at the back of the house – particularly a tallish, orange-haired individual whom we called 'Tom Long', a name off a tobacco-packet. We also discovered by experiment in Richmond itself that a German mark would get you twenty Gold Flake from a chromium-plated machine in Hill Street.

As for Philip Connard, he was not a buffer but rather what is called 'a nice old boy'. We went to tea with him once. He had an elderly-seeming housekeeper who gave us bread and butter, dark damson jam and slices of cake. His first-floor drawing-room was lighter and airier and more negligently arranged than ours. His view of the river was similar but seemed jollier. It may have been my mother's idea, this visit. Perhaps he wanted to paint her, or she wanted him to. Augustus John had found her attractive; Epstein had done her head – a bronze that found its way to Australia. I know of no John painting or drawing of her, but his *Madame Suggia* reminded me of her. She had a sort of pride which only now helps to make sense of the irritating way people used to claim to notice a similarity between my face and hers. As a child I hated being told I looked like her, but now I see the pride, which must have been intensified by my dislike of the suggestion; and I remember too how very sensitive she was to any unpleasant smell. She could smell bugs, mice, failures in personal cleanliness, a hint of a taint in food, the very beginnings of staleness. People's houses, like people themselves, all smell different. She was fastidious.

Charles Graham's cards amuse me but this time I have had to send him a card with a quotation on it that does fit. I've sent him one from Binham Priory and found a rhyme to go with it. It's a fragment of medieval painting. The caption on the back reads:

> Christ as the Man of Sorrows. Mediaeval painting showing through the later painted black-letter text from Cranmer's Bible of 1539 – I Timothy 6, x–xii. ('For the love of money is the root of all evil' – King James version.)

The rhyme I found is an illustrative quotation from *The Shorter Oxford English Dictionary*, citing an early instance of the word 'usury' in English. It is dated 1303.

> To whom that usery ys lefe,
> Gostely he ys a thefe.

I wonder when usury officially ceased to be a sin.

15

I sit and look out of the window and wonder if I ever felt happy or at ease in the company of my sister Sally. She was born on 29 November 1924, a little over seven months after my parents were married (17 April 1924) at Chelsea Register Office. My guess – and children who are not told have to guess – is that these dates are significant; that Sally's advent caused my parents to marry, and thus cut short my mother's promising career on the stage. My father was no Victorian throwback, but he had his pride, and he smarted from not being employed to exercise his undoubted talents as designer, lighting expert and so forth. This made him hypersensitive to what might be said were he to depend in any way on my mother for income. He would hardly hear of her working, though early in 1924 and again in 1925 he had little choice but to resign himself to my mother's appearing in Nigel Playfair's

Beggar's Opera production in New York and London. She played Lucy Lockit, pregnant both times.

Sally's other offence was that she was a girl. About this I do not have to guess: my mother was visibly happier when surrounded by her sons. And one of the saddest and best-remembered tunes of my childhood was my sister's cry, 'The boys! It's always the boys!' 'The boys' is how my mother referred to us whenever planning an outing or an afternoon.

There was some dreadful tale of cruelty undergone by her at the hands of a nanny in Highgate, where Jeffrey was born; something involving a hot iron. I don't know the truth of it and never did; but cruelty did go on, of that I'm sure. My mother was cruel to her, whoever else may have been, and in ways that didn't always show. I can't forget something she said to Sally when we were about eleven and twelve. There had been some sort of quarrel between Sally and 'the boys' and my mother had humiliated her and made her cry. She cried like me, with features crumpled like candle-wax when it melts; and she took a long time to stop, as I did. We were going somewhere, to a party I think, dressed up, clean and tidy. After a couple of hours Sally was still gloomy-looking.

'Now then, Sally dear, cheer up!'

Sally gave a look into the middle distance as if to say that the world was irreparably damaged, and then sniffed and compressed her lips.

'And smile! You can look very nice when you smile.'

This is the sort of thing I can hardly bear to recall, even fifty-four years later. Because Sally was actually beautiful, and there was my mother, probably looking stunning herself, and determined when abroad with her offspring to make a good impression, not to say a dazzling one. Even at this point the nearest my mother can get to saying something encouraging is to tell her that she *can* look 'very nice' *when* she smiles.

I don't speak of Sally's beauty from my own knowledge or experience, or informed by any member of my family. This is what was told me by outsiders, sometimes strangers to me; people who remember her at fourteen and at twenty and at nine or ten. Gideon Cohen got back to England from Canada before I did and went to see my mother in Lansdowne Walk. He was concerned when I told him I had run away in 1942 and hadn't seen her or spoken to her for three years. He told me when I saw him in 1980 or so that he thought Sally beautiful, a lovely girl, and if he hadn't been married. . . . He trailed off, smiling.

With the sole exception of Bunce Court, where I didn't see very much of Sally, we were always at separate, single-sex schools whose terms did not always precisely coincide. In the holidays she was often doing things with other people. She had mysterious friendships with girls like Paula Mason, Ann Jelinek, Audrey Hodgson, mostly sophisticated and superior relationships that made my mutually respectful and amusing adventures with village boys at Milford – brought to an end by my mother because they were 'rough' – or with Bill and Nog Bryant at Norman's Bay, or with Peter Hodgson, Audrey's tall and raw-boned brother, seem very callow and unrefined. We tended to do things: Sally and her friends talked – we referred to it as chattering or gossiping or 'mothers' meetings'.

But when my mother began to get a lot of work from ENSA, singing to the troops or more likely their officers, since her repertoire was classical rather than popular, and I was taken away from Westminster, I shared the house in Lansdowne Walk with Sally between my stay at the Reeses' and my jobs in Kingston and Esher. Things changed. My mother was away for a week or two at a time. Sally was a student at RADA. She had what to me were important friends, even beautiful and amusing ones. She did not mind my coming to parties with her where people smoked and drank and danced, and were witty and outspoken and 'madly gay' – nothing to do with homosexuality in the early forties.

The war and the blackout, even the air raids, added to the sparkle as black velvet enhances diamonds. At one party near Baker Street I met the much-admired young poet Timothy Corsellis, who was just about to go and get shot down like Hugh Clarke. John Pudney in his best-known poem was to call these young men 'Johnny head-in-air'. Timothy sat on a sofa quietly in the midst of the laughter and music and scent and swirl of skirts, and composed – 'a *postcard* to his *mother*!' a girl exclaimed with a sort of wondering respect. He was or seemed to me immensely kind and wise and charming. He must have been twenty-two or -three.

Coming back in taxis at all hours, often with a friend of Sally's – Kay Bush, whose family lived in Harrow, or Penny Keach, braver and more outrageous than Kay but more of a loner and perhaps more of a sufferer – Sally and I were allies: we both felt huge relief that my mother had not cut short a tour to be with her darlings. We both hated her more than we could conveniently express. Kay Bush kissed me goodnight, perhaps she was a bit drunk. I went to bed with what the popular songs called 'stars in my eyes', blissfully happy; and woke up next morning starving for another sign. She said she might drop in at Coventry Street Corner House – another of my father's successes – after her classes.

Once or twice she actually did, but almost always with Sally. I'm not sure how much of a nuisance I may have become – cramping, as my mother would have put it, Sally's style. I think not much of a nuisance. I was very wide awake by this time as well as careful not to act too young. I was ready for any kind of deviousness and deceit. We were a little like inmates of a debtors' prison – 'Duly let out a'nights to steal for fees', in Swift's phrase – at any rate I was. We both wanted to be free; as free as the pigeons on the roofs in springtime, as free as the lilt of all those songs they played at parties:

> You leave me breathless – that's all I can say:
> I can't say any more; you take my breath away.

Part Two

16

Woo't weep? woo't fight? woo't fast? woo't tear thyself?
Woo't drink up eisel? eat a crocodile?

It was for Kay Bush that I was waiting; in the foyer at Lyons Corner House, Coventry Street. She had certainly, I thought, played a dark and creamy Ophelia in her bedroom at Kenton, Harrow, Middlesex; she might even have played her at RADA. What attracted me to her was her kindness and her love of life and her willingness to laugh. That she was good-looking goes without saying. I didn't know then what I know now: almost all young women are good-looking. In those days I was not so easy to please; I thought I had 'standards' and didn't realize that these had been set up by the advertising people. In any case Kay met all the aesthetic demands I might have made of a love-object.

I stood in the foyer wearing my only suit, my back to some counter or other, and felt my legs beginning to ache and my hope dying away. It was a risky thing to do because there was always the possibility of being accosted by some cruising homosexual. I could fend them off if I saw them coming by sending them a freezing look and turning away. In fact I think the freezing look was what I intended but seldom if ever accomplished – it needed courage I couldn't quite muster. Occasionally I would get sneaked up on and actually spoken to, and this was very disconcerting. I had to keep watch on both sets of doors in case Kay should arrive at one of them and not see me. Her arrival included, in my imagination, a shower of doves and rose petals. I'd done this before. It was a grisly way of spending time.

She had said in answer to my rather urgent questioning – I tried hard to disguise the urgency – that she might be in the Corner House one afternoon. I had no better offers, and no more promising covert to scour for game. In 1941 I was shaving no more than twice a week; I thought I looked hopelessly young and soft-faced.

Coventry Street had a brown-uniformed hall porter or chucker-out in those days, a very large and interestingly ugly individual with little bright-blue eyes, florid cheeks and a blue chin. His eyebrows had a curve to them both merry and malicious. I saw him conferring with a small, neatly dressed, grey-suited man, and shooting a deadly blue glance in my direction. He nodded and bowed to his superior and then stepped towards me. My stomach feeling hollow, I turned in the opposite direction and craned slightly to verify my (affected) impression that I had noticed an acquaintance, when suddenly he was standing unpleasantly close at my side, saying: 'And what are yoo doing?'

Already too indignantly I was spluttering something to the effect that I was waiting for someone, a girl actually.

'I've 'ad my eye on yoo,' says he. 'You'd better 'op it, sonny. We don't want your sort in 'ere.'

17

The most encouraging snatch of conversation I heard in HM Prison, Norwich, where I spent three weeks as a 'peace prisoner' in 1984, took place between a top-floor convict and a screw. I don't know what they had been arguing about, but as I passed them standing on the stairs at the level beneath the top floor the lag said in the familiar tones of mock indignation: 'It's all right for *you*. You only work 'ere. I *live* 'ere!' They were both laughing after that.

Most books about Soho, even the ones with nice photographs, irritate me because they seem to be aimed at, if they don't actually emanate from, people who are besotted with what is called success, and have an almost superstitious respect for money. Their 'Sohos' rapidly fill up with the famous and the well-off, most of whom I should describe as privileged tourists, occasional users of the facilities, people really insulated from what Soho is or may be.

My first sight of the old resort, like my brother Jeffrey's a few years on, was obtained on an errand for my mother, to buy proper spaghetti or ravioli or tomato purée for her. In the course of one of these errands I must have slowed down and looked about me. People stood on the pavement and talked outside the Bar Italia and outside Parmigiani's on the corner of Frith Street and Old Compton Street. There were still yellow horse-drawn Carlo and Gatti ice-carts, traces of straw, nosebags and horse-dung. At any moment London rain on asphalt and tarmac might give way to continental sunshine.

The war closed the Continent. After Dunkirk Dean Street and Old Compton Street were suddenly full of Free French and Canadians, some Poles, some Australians. 'Clubs' appeared on unlikely first floors. Victor Berlemont, Gaston's father, was a more proper object of affection than Charles de Gaulle, though de Gaulle's poster – *Nous avons perdu une bataille: nous n'avons pas perdu la guerre!* – was stuck up in both bars of the York Minster, and there seemed to be no more anti-Nazi place in London.

I began to return late from those errands. Coleman Cohen the tobacconist sold the same Celtique cigarettes as I'd been given by mobilizing poilus on my solitary train journey. E. Ruh didn't mind serving me black coffee at his horseshoe-shaped bar in Frith Street a little nearer to Romilly Street, or mind my staying there far beyond the time a small black takes to drink, poring over Gautier's *Émaux et camées*, and wondering if any of the foreign-looking girls would speak to me. I couldn't speak to them. There's a piece of pavement on the north side of Old Compton Street that is associated so strongly with Gautier that either seems to conjure up the other – at any rate the poem always makes the place appear:

Que tu me plais dans cette robe
Qui te déshabille si bien
Faisant jaillir ta gorge en globe
Montrant tout nu ton bras paiën!

A few steps from this spot was a Spanish café where a young Englishwoman who looked tired and sulky did the waiting, and a youngish silent Spaniard surveyed – all he was monarch of, I suppose – from behind the till.

When did I begin to sweep the gutter with my eyes for half-crowns? I certainly knew what to do with half a crown or its equivalent. Coleman Cohen sold Mexican cigarettes (too harsh), American cigarettes (too expensive), Russian cigarettes (amusing but not satisfying), cheroots of various provenances, and Havana cigars of the kind Bruce and I had stolen from the amazing veneered trolley of which Sir William Mallinson the timber merchant had made a present to my father. ECHTE HAVANA CIGARREN. VERGEWISSERN SIE SICH DASS DAS SIEGEL DER KUBANISCHEN REGIERUNG SICH AUF DIESER KISTE BEFINDET. This label or seal looked like money itself. Coleman Cohen also had a beautiful brass gas jet with a small yellow and blue flame, on which you could light a cigarette.

For a long time, certainly all through the late forties and fifties, buying cigarettes or tobacco at Coleman Cohen's was one of the first things I did on arriving in Soho, whether from an outlying part of London, or the country, or abroad. As I begin to see it now, Soho was home. It was the village where I was known. After being taken once to eat at Chez Filliez, Frith Street, by Harold Alston, I suggested to Michael Nesbitt that we have one really good meal there. The third time I went to Chez Filliez was to work there as a kitchen porter, to be called 'boy' by its admirable chef, and to drink a twice-daily, long-handled pot – the kind in which they made zabaglione – of mild beer fetched from the York Minster by another 'boy', older than I, a commis waiter from upstairs. And the last time I went there was to arrive for work one morning and to find that it had been bombed during the night.

Those first days in Soho I pretended not to be English in the same way, or rather for the same reason, as I had pretended to be so idiotically well-born in the Brighton tobacconist's with Michael. As a foreigner, preferably French, I would be able to smoke and drink precociously; even associate with women, I hoped. I would be free to be continentally gloomy and doom-ridden, rather than being a sulky schoolboy, prone to tears. Wally, the barman in the Helvetia, would serve me; I might be a refugee perhaps.

After working all day in the basement kitchen at Chez Filliez I was free to go. The afternoon break from three to five was not much use except to moon and mooch and drink coffee. The kitchen was very sweaty, whether I was standing at the washing-up sinks or carrying coal for the range. The vegetable chef seemed to take a piss on the coal now and then, so I got it done quickly to avoid spending too long in the chilly dark area below the pavement, and returned to the brutal task of cleaning the tinned insides of the big copper saucepans with sand and vinegar and my bare hands, or during lunch and dinner doing industrial quantities of washing up. On a pay-night I'd have four or five pounds, and the food was really good, unlike the food given to kitchen porters in bigger places.

Thrown out of my father's Coventry Street Corner House, or at least physically propelled through its doors on to the pavement of Coventry Street, I spoke to a policeman who explained to me that they were within their rights, it was private property, there was nothing he could do. I walked blindly round the corner into Rupert Street, and turned into Rupert Court, by the Blue Posts, which was luckily deserted. I don't know where I went after that. Possibly into E. Ruh's Café Bar. I liked his solemn, lopsided face. I knew he wouldn't tell me to cheer up, it might never happen.

18

I don't know, apart from loneliness and a kind of despair of human comfort, how I began my brief and unsuccessful career as a male prostitute or rent boy. I'm not sure even how long it lasted. Perhaps five or six weeks. I feel sure it started at some time soon after my being ejected from Coventry Street Corner House. Eight or ten men and boys may have been involved, and I remember most of them.

One, the least alarming, was an army subaltern on his way to North Africa. Clean shaven, pink-faced, brown-eyed, he bought me a drink in the York Minster. His immaculate dark-brown leather wallet was charged with apparently new pound notes. His Sam Browne was highly polished, his uniform well cut. I rather liked his politeness and timidity; besides, he thought I was French. I told him no, I lived in London. He looked a bit sad and lost. I suppose he was sad with longing, really. I didn't at the time make the comparison, but it seems odd now to think that he was seven or eight years older than my fifteen years, yet I saw him as someone needing protection.

He was a little uneasy, and indeed I can see that his wishes involved a court-martial offence, so I decided to take him home. Why was I so cool? We got a taxi to 19 Lansdowne Walk and I took him upstairs; up the tastefully carpeted stairs and into my bedroom under the roof with the sage-green faded carpet, the portable gramophone and the green eiderdown. He seemed a bit large, close to; he kissed me gently. Lying on the bed, on my eiderdown, he pressed himself against me, almost it seemed weeping; and soon came, was a little happier, and left – to get another taxi, I expect.

I forget what I did with the money, and can't remember how much it was. I still felt sorry for him. He didn't know what he was doing, I felt, or where he was going. I didn't want him to get stupidly killed somewhere.

A far more frightening experience was when I was picked up late at night in Cavendish Square by two young men who were, they told me, fire-watching. They took me down some area steps next to the Broadwood Pianoforte Company, into a basement office with a camp-bed, and proceeded with much joking and a little pain to have their way with me. That is to say, one of them did. I wasn't too sure what the other was doing besides making tea. Observing, perhaps. At all events, having both suffered and committed the crime, I took myself off feeling bedraggled and beaten, thinking I might feel better when I'd had a shit. In fact I didn't feel better for a long time in my mind; probably not until I was safe in the heterosexual, slightly puritanical arms of the Communist Party. But that came later. In the meantime, I had become a sort of pariah.

I was fifteen, but what did my age matter? I had committed . . . and not in another land; and I was still alive. I was walking about spreading my own darkness and fear. It took a courageous or an unimaginative café waitress to say to me: cheer up darlin'. Certain old men, Wally in the Helvetia for instance, with his wheezing, whispery voice, were gloomily kind, and appeared not to notice how damned I was.

Not for the first time I felt that I was serving a sentence; not imprisoned but forced to undergo a period of humiliation, and wondering when it would be over, when I'd be free. The sky was indifferent, the pavements passive, the houses belonged to other people, and other people were unknown and unknowing. I had deeply offended the lot of them, and I was determined not to care.

Strangely, it was a pair of young scallywags, one of whom I'd met when we worked as extras on a film (British National, Elstree) called *The Common Touch*, who came to my help. Their protector was a man in St James's Street, a person of rank, I'd better call him. The boys were barely undergraduates, their accents top-drawer. They played with me lasciviously but quite kindly; there was no question of the dreaded crime. They did schoolboy things, conversed mischievously and teasingly, and exploded in mirth. Our meetings generally took place in a bachelor, rather Forsyteish flat, where there were well-framed prints and photographs and a polished mahogany sideboard containing orange squash and soda water which we all consumed liberally. The man in whose apartments we spent our time together was a person of taste. He both amused and slightly horrified me when in pursuit of his collector's enthusiasm he referred to a dealer off Bond Street as 'my Jew': 'I must go and see my Jew, and see what he has found for me this week.' His speech was very clear and level. He was impeccably well mannered and not at all effeminate. He said to me one evening in French: 'It appears that you are really somewhat uncertain as to your sexual orientation.' I agreed gratefully, not wishing to hurt his feelings by entirely rejecting homosexuality. Something clear and serious seemed to hold him together, straighter than most people of whatever orientation. A sort of correctness. Not that he was unsympathetic; but I noticed that he was a privileged person who appeared never to have thought about, much less doubted, his right to comfort, money, position and so on. The clarity and correctness – devoid of any trace of anxiety to be 'correct' – were obviously there to imitate or emulate.

It seemed at last no longer necessary to pursue this brief and rather stupid excursion into homosexual adventure. I was free. All I had to do was get myself out of my moral lethargy and financial difficulties. There was really no excuse in those days for being without money if one were healthy.

19

It's Sunday, 16 February 1992 and my niece Lisa comes to tea. Tea is a lean and threadbare version of what I was accustomed to at her age – she's twenty-two. We begin by going for a short, cold walk, up Mill Lane, along the side of the bare and windswept fields towards Park Common, and back down another lane to this street again. Her shiny boots have mud on them and she takes them off. We finish up the Lapsang Souchong in the cut-glass jar and sip it in the warmth of this room. It is very cold outside and very warm in here.

What's nourishing, though, is that we talk a lot: about her work and my work; her fellow-students; the pink paint on Battersea Bridge; why people in London don't smile; her work in journalism before she began studying picture restoration; the NUJ and the IOJ. She's reading about boys' boarding-schools and the fear of homosexuality. Because of her youth and good looks, and her openness and intelligence, and the fact that I like her mother, I find it easy to talk to her. I even find myself saying what has never occurred to me.

'I think the reason that men in our culture are so fiercely against homosexual practices is that they regard women as definitely second class. They're terrified of being *turned into a woman* by being 'had' by a homosexual.'

'It's frightening,' says Lisa.

'But you see what I mean. The danger is that you become what you fundamentally despise – you know, the "weaker" sex, the inferior sex, all that!'

She raises her eyebrows as if hearing something new. 'Yes, I think you're right.' Then she goes on reading, and I begin to remember a short, funny exchange with Dan Farson in the Colony Room five years ago.

Dan and I are on quite polite and friendly terms these days, particularly since I told him about the gay librarian of an institution I once attended who would stand at the urinal and say to a student in the next stall: 'Now let me see, aren't you the young man who has the Longfellow out?' At the time of the Colony Room conversation things were a little less comfortable. Dan was making some huge unbridled generalization about females when I said to him: 'That's not a very nice thing to say about women, Dan.'

'Oh I know you, Oliver,' says Dan. 'You're like Michael Law. You're an Honorary Woman!'

'Oh! Thank you!'

I couldn't wait to tell Michael after that. I don't see him very often, though. I miss him from the fifties' places: the Caves de France, the York Minster, the Gargoyle. I think I must have become much less tolerant of noisy places lately. Michael Law is elegant and self-effacing. I think I must write to him, but I almost never do.

20

I was told, I don't know how reliably, that my father had had a hand in the design of some detail of the cockpit of the Vickers-Supermarine seaplane which in 1931 won Britain the Schneider Trophy outright, and from which the Spitfire was developed. But I don't know at whose suggestion or by whose influence I started work in the drawing office of Hawker Aircraft in Kingston upon Thames. Soon after I started there, lodging with a friendly, red-faced, chain-smoking milk roundsman at a small house with one of the few tolerable landladies in my entire experience, the drawing office was moved to one of Sally's old boarding-schools, Claremont, so I got another landlady in Esher about whom my memory is entirely blank.

I did practically no drawing at all apart from an hour or two's training each week, about which I remember little beyond the anonymity, I may even say the blankness, of the small aircraft parts I tried to draw, and the importance placed on giving the pencil point what was called a 'chisel edge'. Most of the time I had to take drawings from place to place, and obtain blueprints from a huge machine that smelt of ammonia and had a very bright light inside it. The prints were not actually blue like the old ones in the files. This was a more modern system that produced dark mauve lines on paper which should have been white but which was generally of a pale mauve tint. I shared for a time a small office in the neo-classical pediment of the front of the building – at about that level anyway – with a girl called Almina de Carvalho who neither looked nor sounded Portuguese. We moved to a part of the building that Sally had told me about, in a previous life it seemed: Clive's Bath. This was fairly cluttered with metal filing cabinets and a Gestetner duplicator, but the same marble steps led down into it that the toga'd Clive of India, as I imagined him, had used when it was filled with brownish water heated at vast expense by domestics, using oaks from the estate or coal from Newcastle.

I went out once or twice with one of the tracers, a quiet and lovely young person who wanted to be a dancer; but it came – after some ardour on my part and shyness on hers – to nothing. Kenneth Cheeseman, a designer who worked for Pilkington's, and who had been a protégé of my father's, came to Esher one weekend and stayed at the Bear Hotel. He was an extremely shy and repressed person, quite immaculate except that his fingernails were bitten down to the quicks. He told me stories about his digs in Prescot and his work at St Helen's. He went everywhere on a much-prized motor cycle, a Brough Superior. He was an occasional painter and there was some talk of art.

Two people I met in Esher were to have some importance for me. One was Hugh Forsyth, who became a copywriter and perhaps some sort of librarian at Burroughs Wellcome. He was quite learned and literary, a great admirer of Dylan Thomas. His father had been one of the first Freudian analysts in England. The other was Mr Cotterell, a lecturer at Morley College and a Marxist. I attended some classes he gave about drama, and took part in the reading of a number of modern plays, of which the only one I recall is *The Adding Machine* by Elmer Rice. This was an angry left-wing piece about a city wage-slave in New York which must have lacked the humanity of *Death of a Salesman* but may have encouraged Miller in the writing of it.

Mr Cotterell – it amuses me now that there was nothing remarkable in 1941 about my not knowing his first name – was dry-spoken, reddish haired, kindly. I don't think he approved of my working at Hawker's, but he showed no curiosity about the place. As for me, the word Typhoon never crossed my lips until 1943 when I was in uniform; but I remember my mother talking about the Beaufighter the day she returned from Coltishall, where the officers' mess had been captivated by her singing. In the event, neither aircraft was very successful. I think they were over-powered and difficult to handle.

Mr Cotterell passed me a Communist Party pamphlet or two, and I went to a couple of meetings, or at least intended to. But I may have been sidetracked by again meeting Peter Hodgson, the brother of my sister's friend Audrey. He had no ideas at all about politics. His father was an irascible ex-army major who worked for the Birmingham Small Arms Company (BSA) and his mother was a sweet, rather fragile woman who once gave us pink gins and laughed like a young girl. Peter had an absurd bicycle with a small two-stroke engine which he called 'the old fart-and-flyback'. But he took me to a party or two where I met Mr Yate's daughter, with whom I did not get far. Her father was an architect in Great Marlborough Street and offered me a job in his drawing office. So I returned to London, having had enough of Esher and Claremont, and not feeling that my departure would even be noticed by my employers.

My salary at the architect's office was a little better but not good. I did no drawing but spent most of the time surveying West End buildings: something to do with war damage. I ate in workmen's cafés and went to Morley College once a week. I read American novels and Russian novels and anything else I could find – Aldous Huxley, Virginia Woolf, Evelyn Waugh. I found one of my father's old ring-leaf books with unlined paper in it and began to sketch again: Georgian doorways with fanlights; a wrought-iron gate of Florentine design in Lansdowne Road; my own feet in sandals which I remember putting up on a bench in the King's Head and Eight Bells near the Albert Bridge and drawing very carefully, reaching without looking at it for my beer as I worked on the sketch. I was both disquieting and a little absurd in those days. Perhaps I still am: but then, I am sure, it showed.

21

I've forgotten the date of the air raid during which the bomb fell higher up Lansdowne Walk, but we were all at home in the basement kitchen and I felt the floor rise and fall in a way I did not understand until years later I saw some newsreel film of American daylight bombing. The sun in those films may have been very low or not; but what was clearly visible was the shock wave across the ground spreading from the bomb bursts like the rings made by stones dropped in water, only very much faster. We went out to have a look. There was still a column of dust where the house had been, ghostly in bright moonlight. Searchlight beams waved vaguely or clustered on nothing. Gunfire still echoed. We were told to come indoors because of the shrapnel from anti-aircraft shells.

By the time the Germans had reached Leningrad and captured Kiev I had decided that I had to act. I joined the ATC – the Air Training Corps – which had a drill hall near Kensington Park Road, and soon after that, overstating my age by a year, I volunteered for aircrew training in the RAFVR. In the same week I applied to join the Communist Party of Great Britain. I was at first advised to join the Young Communist League, but somehow managed to avoid the category of youth – I loathed the idea of anything junior – and went to my first meeting in a room above a newsagent's shop in Notting Hill Gate. By the spring of 1942 I had been to RAF Halton and survived tests for pilot training, including one about 'courage and determination' which mystified us all because we weren't sure exactly how these qualities were assessed. I think I decided that our resistance to being talked out of 'flying and fighting in the air' was what got us through, and that the test was simply a piece of attempted browbeating by the interviewing officer.

The local communists ran meetings on Sunday evenings outside Notting Hill Gate underground station – the entrance in Pembridge Gardens – and my first attempts at public speaking were very exciting, fuelled by hatred of the Nazis and I suspect by personal feelings of anger. When on one of these evenings I noticed my mother at the edge of the crowd, I was well into my stride and simply flicked past her angry eyes to address another segment of the audience. The subject was almost certainly the desirability of a 'second front' in Europe against the German Army.

On my return to Lansdowne Walk I had to listen to a long scolding about 'Bolshevism' and 'that type of person' and the fact that I was still very much a minor. Who did I think I was, etc. I didn't try to justify myself; I was beginning to realize that, so to speak, I thought I was myself.

I still could not get fixed up with a girl-friend, though there was an almost possible girl of sixteen or seventeen round the corner in Clarendon Road. If I had been seventeen myself, instead of barely sixteen. . . . But I knew it was extremely unlikely, really; so I was all the more bitter at my mother's dismissal of her as 'quite a nice little thing'. I already suspected that my mother preferred me to associate with homosexual men than with women of any age or size. I could even remember a bus ride back from Menton to Roquebrune during which she'd told me, with polite and grateful smiles at him, to sit on the lap of a gentleman in white trousers, who was then for a second or two grossly familiar, and who never stopped smiling.

Our last confrontation was over the hours I kept. It had made me feel sick when she told me that I was now 'the man of the house'. But when one morning she said 'This is my house and I will not have you coming in at whatever time pleases you', I said something rebellious like 'Oh, won't you?' and received a sudden slap that rattled my teeth.

The next thing I knew was that I had raised my arm – more as a guard than in order to strike her, I think – and she was saying to me: 'Don't you dare! Don't you dare raise your arm to me!'

I went out through the scullery and up the area steps knowing that I was going to leave: my feet pushed it all down and behind me as if for the last time. If I was a brute, I'd be a brute.

For a few days I waited, gradually packing an old leather suitcase of my father's with a few of his old shirts and some of my clothes; then, one afternoon, I slipped out of the house, thinking there was no one else in.

The weight of the suitcase became intolerable when to my horror I realized that my mother was following me. I ran down the spiral stairs at Holland Park tube station and hid in an alcove along the platform. I heard her come down the steps from the lift and stop to scan the platform. When the train arrived I got on it alone.

Arriving at Jack and Topsy Clark's mews flat near Devonshire Street, off Portland Place, I was once more among the beautiful people. Jack must have married Topsy at the beginning of the war. She was very kind and seemed more amused than anything at my escape. I don't know how I found them. I must have met Jack somewhere political, and remembered that old copy of the *Daily Worker* and his explanation of capitalism. Anyway they were very kind and friendly. On my first day of freedom I found a job and somewhere to live, and plunged into my new life as if I had acquired gills and would now never swim any way but under water.

I got a job as a packer at Central Books in Parton Street, Red Lion Square – a wholesale and retail bookshop run by an Irishman, Bagenal Harvey, who as manager was responsible to the Central Committee of the Communist Party in King Street, Covent Garden. I took a room in a shabby hotel in Bernard Street, near Russell Square tube station. It was on the top storey and had linoleum on the floor and a rag rug next to the rather shapeless bed. The bedclothes seemed limp and perhaps slightly damp. When opened, the door came away from the jamb with a sticky sound. There was a modern wash-basin with running water, and a gas ring. The view from the window was mainly of chimneys.

22

The packing bench is covered with lino, smooth and with no possibility of splinters. Behind it on the wall hangs the wrapping paper in big sheets on a rope. Lay a sheet of wrapping paper on the bench, then lay sheets of packing paper on it till you have a good thickness to protect your books, then lay a length of corrugated paper, ribbed side up, from the back to the front of your packing. Build the books in the centre of the corrugated paper. Decide from the quantity whether you are going to have four or five or eight to a layer, then think of bricks and bond them like that. Don't have a crack running right down the pile. Mostly three widths is two lengths, see?

Harry Smolins taught me how to pack. He wore spectacles and had a thin face, a lean jaw, a slightly florid mouth. He was earnest and conscientious. Abe Cohen worked next to me. He was short and stocky and had a cynical manner, but he saved me from a few embarrassing situations, for instance leaving my packing knife inside the parcel, or omitting some small item. Alf Silverman once sent his pipe to Manchester. He was older than most of us, rather philosophical and benevolent. No women worked in the packing-room, but Gwen or Sadie or Marie would come in with orders, and we all had two tea-breaks a day upstairs in the fire-watching room next to the caretaker's flat. Tea-breaks were also the kinds of meetings at which we would hear announcements about 'musters' – that is, mobilization of the whole work-force for the purpose of doing unpaid overtime to shift sudden large quantities of Party leaflets or of a new pamphlet. Occasionally Bagenal would address us on some problem of working methods or standards. Mostly it was tea and gossip and jokes and rumours. We all got along very well, it was a community – not unlike that of a camping organization I came to know thirty years later. But whereas Flysheet Camps is dedicated to child care and education, Central Books was dedicated to anti-Nazi struggle and socialism in all countries. No fundamental contradiction perhaps.

Harry Pollitt in Montague Place, or Harry Pollitt on the plinth of the Nelson Column in Trafalgar Square, gave a certain glamour to the Party. He was a most persuasive and a most passionate speaker, with trade-union and prison experience behind him. He was inimitable, concentrated, dynamic; and he could make people weep. But I studied mainly at Speakers' Corner, Marble Arch. Being impatient and rather narrowly left-wing, I spent less time listening to Bonar Thompson than I should now wish to have done. Michael Foot's description of him in *Debts of Honour* is marvellously evocative. My main tutor was the redoubtable Tony Turner, who spoke from the Socialist Party of Great Britain platform and attracted very large crowds with his rhetoric, his wide and beautiful eyes, and his peculiar gestures – he had a special way of extending his forearms and clapping his hands together pointing away from him as he emphasized points. When I heckled him he swung round towards me, wonderfully maintaining his balance and flow, and said with relish: 'I think we have a little Stalinist in our midst!' He was as much of a star as Bonar Thompson, whom Michael Foot calls 'the Hyde Park Sceptic' – indeed Foot says that from that platform (the SPGB one) he heard 'the purest milk of the word flowing'.

When Bill Balcombe came to Central Books, I began to spend Saturday afternoons putting into practice what little I had learnt.

23

Before I gave away my black-and-white TV set last autumn I noticed among the credits at the end of a *Star Trek* episode the name of Hans Beimler. I began to hear the tune of a somewhat sentimental First World War song about a fallen comrade – instantly recognized by a *Wehrmacht* prisoner with whom I became acquainted at the end of my RAF service – which had been adapted during the Spanish war as a German International Brigade song:

Ich hatt' einen Kameraden
Einen bessern find'st du nicht

Bill Balcombe, who looked a bit like a tall version of Buster Keaton, with long eyelashes and an expression of anxious sincerity, had left a bag of laundry in Philly, as he called it, but had brought an American album of International Brigade songs back from the States with him. He had a long shore leave and spent it working in the packing-room at Central Books. He had a room in Montague Street facing the left forequarter side of the British Museum in which he spent little time. But in this room, nobly proportioned but meanly furnished, he played me his records, which included not only the Hans Beimler song but also a wonderfully gloomy song called 'Die Moor-Soldaten', about forced labour in the Third Reich.

Bill and I spent a lot of time together, eating lunch at Vince's, a friendly, cheap restaurant in Eagle Street, near Kingsway, and sometimes having a meal at the British Restaurant on the south side of Russell Square, where lunch was even cheaper, though very much like school food. Rationing made cooking at home difficult, so eating out was the answer. Besides, there were only two sorts of landladies, apparently: mean ones and mad ones. Bill's was the mad sort, he said. He was wonderfully generous and vague himself, and he and Bagenal and I did a certain amount of drinking when Christmas came along and Central Books had a staff party at a Greek restaurant near the top of Shaftesbury Avenue. This was, however, exceptional. Most of the time we worked hard and drank tea and took politics seriously. We were the two activists of Holborn Branch Communist Party. Everyone else lived in Hackney or Stepney. Ken and Gwen in accounts lived in Sussex.

I don't know how Holborn Branch got into such a low state, but I think it was the result of losing all its members employed in government departments, and particularly the advertising people and journalists who worked at the Ministry of Information. These were now all 'undercover' Party members. They left behind them in the official Holborn Branch what Bill and I derisively and probably unfairly labelled 'bureaucrats'.

The two of us gloried in our youthful enthusiasm, muscle and imagination. We picked up the worn but sturdily constructed red-painted folding platform – about three and a half feet above contradiction – from the Party offices in Great James Street every Saturday afternoon, and carried it and a suitcase full of 'literature' to Denmark Street, Charing Cross Road: Tin Pan Alley did no business after lunchtime on Saturdays. Bill was Literature Secretary, I was Propaganda Secretary. We were properly elected officials of our branch; but we regarded that as a joke, simply another piece of bureaucracy. In fact I'm sure that working at Central Books was a sort of guarantee of our political reliability. 'King Street' would not have countenanced the employment of any but the most irreproachably pure communists – or so we all thought.

We set up our Saturday afternoon meetings at the corner of Denmark Street and Charing Cross Road, almost opposite Foyles. Bill introduced 'this afternoon's speaker' while I pushed out leaflets and sold pamphlets. When he'd made the introductory remarks, I took his place on the platform and treated a growing audience – there was a shortage of entertainment in those days, or else this was free entertainment – to a harangue about the conduct of the war and the aims of the Communist Party, calling for a second front in Europe to relieve the pressure of the *Wehrmacht* on the Russian front, and for the removal of the current ban on the *Daily Worker*. Then I took questions; and then Bill asked for a collection of money for our cause.

I presume that it was at one of these meetings that I first attracted the attention of the Special Branch or whichever undercover policing organization it was that followed my progress through the rest of my RAF career. I certainly had my name and the number on the back of my silver RAFVR badge taken; and at Heaton Park, Manchester, where I spent six months instead of the normal two or three waiting for a ship to Canada, I was told by a WAAF corporal who was a *Daily Worker* reader that my commanding officer and the RAF police were corresponding about my 'case'. I experienced further long delays at Moncton, New

Brunswick, which gave me an opportunity to explore eastern Canada a bit, and possibly saved my life. I should not have felt grateful for this at the time.

I remember little of the details of these meetings in Denmark Street. On one bright afternoon an old man walking up past Foyles on the opposite side of Charing Cross Road shouted: 'We want Jesus, not Lenin!' He was bearded and wild-looking and I rather liked him for the strange interruption. One afternoon we collected over nine pounds in pennies and sixpences, and the following week the ban on the *Daily Worker* was lifted. The sight of a growing crowd with its slight movement and murmur always intoxicated me slightly. And one Saturday afternoon a really handsome young woman asked me to come and have coffee afterwards.

24

We all know about the power of cheap music, and it is a long time since I began not to mind, and even to enjoy it. I liked it at Sally's parties, and I liked it in Canada and when I returned to work out my remaining time in the RAF, and I went to as many dances as possible. For a time in Soho and in Suffolk I took against it and would listen to nothing but the Third Programme, having become very serious or snobbish. Now I can listen to anything, provided it is not too loud. But the power of popular proverbs is more unpleasant and harder to shake off, especially living alone. The idea that 'the Devil finds work for idle hands to do', for example, is really nasty as well as probably heretical, implying as it does that God can't fill the vacuum. I've always liked the title of Byron's first volume of poems – *Hours of Idleness* – and sensed a slant reference to it at the beginning of *The True Confession of George Barker*:

> Today, recovering from influenza,
> I begin, having nothing worse to do,
> This autobiography that ends a
> Half of my life I'm glad I'm through.

A young person's seeming obsession with sex may be intensified by frustrations of various kinds; even by the need to love and be loved. It has nothing to do with the Devil in, so to speak, broad daylight on a Monday morning.

I had fantasized fairly continuously about girls and women ever since I was thirteen, but since the excitement of the summer of 1940 I had had only few and unsatisfactory encounters with them. While fire-watching at Central Books I had been welcomed into the arms of a girl with red hair, whom I blamed probably quite unjustifiably for giving me crab-lice: I imagine the blankets in the fire-watchers' room were seldom cleaned. There had also been a picaresque adventure one pay-night in the West End, before I ran away from home. The rogue of the story was a distinguished, affable, grey-haired gentleman who bought me a drink at Ward's in Shaftesbury Avenue and asked me whether I was interested in girls. 'Well yes, of course,' I said. 'What do you mean?' He explained that he had a sort of open invitation to a house in Maida Vale where several girls lived. 'Not prostitutes,' he said. 'Thoroughly nice girls, but – you know – ready for anything. Very friendly.' The odd thing was that he closely resembled a retired American naval officer to whom we had all been introduced at the Christian Science church in Marsham Street, as respectable as, say, the Chase Manhattan Bank.

The commodore, I'll call him, hailed a taxi and off we went. In the cab he got two pounds ten shillings from me. It was customary, he said, to give the girls a present. I mentally demoted him by a couple of ranks. When we reached the house it appeared that he was known there, though the reception he got was a bit *distrait*: it seemed he wasn't expected. Two young women left us waiting in a sort of anonymous drawing-room, and while they were out of the room he asked me which 'girl' I preferred. One of them was taller than the other and dark-haired; she had looked straight at me and smiled. 'The dark one,' I said.

I insisted on washing before joining the dark one on a large bed. I undressed feeling embarrassed and disturbed. She told me I was very young; then she laughed because I wanted to repeat the performance; and allowed it.

As we were getting dressed we heard the commodore and his 'girl' with raised voices. He was actually shouting very ugly things, and she was being shrill and denunciatory, on a descending scale that seemed to suggest that she had expected the worst from the start. She came into our room saying 'The bastard. The dirty bastard!' The tall dark woman put an arm round her shoulders. She was beginning to cry.

'What's happened?' I asked.

'He's gone, that's what,' said the commodore's companion.

I looked at mine. She shrugged in her blue and white striped linen dressing-gown and said: 'Come on, let's have a cup of tea.' So we went and sat in the kitchen.

'Did you give him any money?'

My heart sank. 'Yes. Two pounds ten.'

'The bastard.'

We started to drink tea, and another, older, woman joined us. I was introduced and asked my age. I smiled confusedly and said seventeen. They all laughed and said I didn't look it, however I acted.

We must have talked for a good while because it was getting light as I walked back to Holland Park. I wished I could live with this woman and somehow take care of her. But when I telephoned her she wouldn't see me. She said her steady boy-friend was back from somewhere and she planned to marry him one day.

25

The young woman who asked me to come and have coffee turned out to be one of the undercover communists. She lived in a modern block of flats in Woburn Place, in which there were several other communists. These included advertising copywriters and designers who were working for the Ministry of Information for the time being. One of them was 'Boogie' Barnes, who had been terribly injured in the bombing of the Café de Paris, and whom I was to meet rather uncomfortably at a dinner given by the Advertising Association in the early sixties, by which time he was a director of Benson's. Another was a brilliant and intense woman called Nella Fox-Edwards, Nella Bowen, a close friend of this young woman, another copywriter. Her name was Jasmine Gordon-Forbes, and she came from Rhodesia. She had not been in London very long: she worked on the *National Geographic Magazine* as art editor, down Charing Cross Road. She was very quick and vivid and direct. I suppose one of the things that interested her about me was that I was young and showed some signs of being educated and – this is the main thing – that I was actually sticking my neck out and *doing* something. She has I think always been a bit impatient and irritable in the face of inactivity. Even now she is always doing something: art, photography, friends, offspring – chivvying someone, looking after someone, gardening, travelling, talking animatedly, writing. I liked her because she was so alive, because she responded to everything: life was too short; there was so much to see and to learn and to do. She made me, busy as I was, active as I was, feel that I had been asleep.

So Jasmine took me in hand, and I was more than grateful. She taught me about lettering, about design, even about T.S. Eliot. She went to the country at weekends to paint, and came back elated or annoyed. She asked me abrupt questions about what I was doing and what I hoped to do. She washed a green sweater of mine and made me smarten up a bit. She even found me a room.

I had got very fed up with my hotel. I disliked the slight dampness and the dark-green linoleum, the stickiness of the black-gloss painted door and the thin window curtains I no more wanted to touch than the grimed and cracked glazing bars of the window. The bed was not inviting, and the stairs began in plum-coloured carpet, stifling, and ended with bare treads at the top, poverty-stricken. While I was there I had contracted both head-lice and scabies at different times; they seemed to intensify the vague sordidness of the place, even though it was not the place that was responsible. Scabies in particular was very common in London in the middle of the war.

The room Jasmine found for me was at 12 Brunswick Square. I had never had such a room, and have never had such a room since. It was very large and high-ceilinged; the balcony ran the whole width of the building past both french windows and in front of the kitchen window. If ever the phrase *piano nobile* was necessary, it was to designate this first floor. The room faced east: the morning sun shone over Brunswick Square itself, and over the Foundling Hospital and Mecklenburgh Square beyond. Below me lived a German or Austrian woman psychiatrist whom I hardly ever saw. There was so little traffic that I could hear the horse-drawn United Dairies' milk-cart all the way to Coram Street with its faint chink of bottles. Under the barrage balloons or under the stars, London was a city that could not escape and had not escaped, but it was still beautiful and you could walk about in it. Bloomsbury at weekends was blissfully quiet.

Jasmine lent me a portable gramophone, a heavy oak box with a carved lid and two little doors in front. On it I played an incomplete set of black-label HMV records of Beethoven's Fifth Symphony, 78s of course, with the second movement missing. It seemed to me all righteous indignation and triumph, and was a great resource. The V-sign symphony. I have wondered a bit since about the enlistment of Beethoven in the anti-Nazi cause. I know that in Hitchcock's *Psycho* I am vastly amused by the way the camera pans round the young man's bedroom, snooping among his possessions, and comes to rest after zooming to a close-up of the record label on *his* turntable: SYMPHONY No. 3 'EROICA'. You know, then, that he's crazy.

26

I don't think I was mad in 1942. In many ways I was happier than I had ever been. I had a job in which I was liked and trusted; I had friends at work; and when Jasmine came into my life so unexpectedly I had a young woman to love. And the room was very important. It was as if I had made a lucky landfall after a rough passage: I could begin to live again after so long trying to survive.

Brunswick Square was a more than satisfactory place to live: I could have people to tea, I could read and write there. Bill Balcombe talked about it at work. Bagenal started asking after 'the palace'. People made smart remarks about 'coffee with Nella Fox-Edwards'. I never mentioned Jasmine's name.

Of course some of what I was doing, though exciting, was not quite in character. It was odd perhaps to have accepted Party discipline and RAF discipline as well. I suppose that the Party was a kind of refuge, an alternative family; this was certainly true of Central Books. And the RAF was intended to be a way of putting my life where my anti-fascist mouth was. There was no question of dying. In Canada I became aware that all of us thought we were immortal, with our slow rolls and loops and steep turns, and our (simulated) engine failures on take off. And if we weren't immortal, there was always this favourite quotation of Lenin's, which I learnt in the packing-room of Central Books:

> Man's dearest possession is life; and since it is given to him to live but once, he must so live as to feel no torturing regrets for years

> without purpose; so live as not to be seared by the shame of a cowardly and trivial past; so live that, dying, he can say: 'All my life and all my strength were given to the noblest cause in the world – the liberation of mankind.'

All I can find wrong with it is that it is not in *The Oxford Dictionary of Quotations* which I have just consulted in order to check it. It comes, I think, from some nineteenth-century Russian author. And God is, as often, implicit.

27

Public speaking was the glamorous end of my activities. At the other was leafletting, which I had first done round council flats in North Kensington, along with chalking slogans at night, using big blocks of doorstep whitening, and keeping a sharp eye out for policemen. In addition, a few of us from the packing-room sold pamphlets at Tottenham Court Road tube station, sometimes next to the pitch of a newspaper seller who for a long time that year shouted nothing but 'Russia's grave news!' in a hoarse and doom-laden voice. When Hutchinson published Ilya Ehrenburg's *The Fall of Paris* at ten shillings and sixpence – the *Stalingrad* pamphlet that sold so fast was priced at tuppence – we found we could sell that, too, on the street. It was almost incredible. The equivalent today would be a novel at £13.99.

Second front rallies in Trafalgar Square would fill it with fifty thousand people. After one of these I had a deserved drink in the York Minster and began to whistle, as was my habit, when a large warrant officer in RAF uniform standing at the bar next to me said: 'Tchaikovsky was a bourgeois composer.' In the ensuing conversation it turned out that he was a musician himself: John Gardner, at that time conductor of Fighter Command Band. I saw him several times before I was myself in uniform, and always expected to hear of him as a composer. He was remarkably intelligent and alive. In fact I heard his Symphony No. 1 on the radio on 23 January 1952, ten years later.

Jasmine and I went to Box Hill on more than one Sunday. We ate once or twice in Soho. But what I remember best was being in her flat in Russell Court, sharing the weekly lamb chops – the meat ration – and reading Eliot and Hopkins. She had a copy of the Simson Shand type book which I used in order to try to learn lettering; my handwriting altered completely because I began to model it on hers which was, I thought, exquisite. She taught me so much in a few months it seemed that she had taught me everything – about life and literature and sex and food and just enjoying things. All I didn't know how to do when the intimacy came to an end was to be without her. Obviously something that started within a fortnight of her twenty-fifth and my seventeenth birthdays could hardly be expected to last. In any case I was committed to overstating my age, or it might not have started at all. I can feel nothing but gratitude now.

28

I was handed my RAF uniform at Lord's cricket ground in April 1943, and found myself sleeping at Viceroy Court, Prince Albert Road, and being marched to breakfast and all other meals at the Zoo. A whoop of monkeys over cool, almost solid scrambled egg. Barrack-room natter and boast. Regional accents. Rumours. 'We're being posted to Scotland, North Wales, Torquay' and so on. Uncomfortable goodbyes at Central Books, and the world seen as nastily different from the very bottom of yet another ladder. Saluting officers was interesting for the first two or three times, but the West End was full of them.

I was lucky to go to No. 2 ITW (Initial Training Wing) in Cambridge. We were billeted at Pembroke College, and ate and had lectures in various other colleges. We had a rowing eight and took part in bump races, scoring a double bump in spite of a good deal of beer-drinking and swimming during our training. Cambridge seemed elegant and beautiful even if marching along King's Parade at 120 paces to the minute, arms swung shoulder high, was neither. My two favourite subjects were aircraft recognition and meteorology. We had a sergeant instructor for aircraft recognition with a wonderfully loud, clear voice whose mnemonic for the Junkers 88 was 'Two bloody great engines, followed by an aeroplane'. As for met., as we called it, I'm still an addict. It's the only thing I miss on television – the map with the isobars – and I'm always slightly surprised and disappointed when people don't know in their bones, as I do, that if you stand with your back to the wind in the northern hemisphere, the area of lower pressure is to your left. But I suppose it's like knowing in what phase the moon is. It's not really bones, of course; it's whether it matters to you. I don't know why it matters to me. I suppose that when people say 'It's none of my business' and shrug like non-voters in an alleged democracy I get irritated and decide to *make* it my business. How can people tell you it's a nice day and be unaware that they live in the solar system?

After many lectures and many parades, and breaking a metatarsal marching in gleaming boots, I went to a flying field called Caxton Gibbet – 'a medieval aerodrome' someone dubbed it – and started flying 'Tigers'. No subsequent flying seems in retrospect so pure. We had to wear goggles, sit on our parachutes and watch out to the left at the appropriate moment where a spring-loaded flap, fixed to a strut between the wings, indicated stalling speed. Flying was strange enough for me to be able to ignore my left-handedness, though having to hold the control column in the right hand made it no easier. To have my left hand on the throttle seemed a quite pleasant idea, by contrast. Having got out of a spin or two, I was allowed to loop the aircraft. My instructor was of course a tremendously important figure, not unlike a prep-school teacher I had had, called Mr Sobey, but more alert. I met him in Cambridge once, drinking, and he told me to (a) stop trying to pick a fight with an American corporal, and (b) have a drink. I went solo in nine hours or so: nothing unusual.

I must have had three or four leaves before I arrived at Heaton Park, Manchester, but I remember none of them clearly. On one of them I went to a photographer's studio in Old Compton Street which advertised its proprietor as THE REMBRANDT OF LONDON. I wanted a picture to give to a young woman I was seeing, and the result was a very dewy version of my face indeed. I took the girl, whose name was Gladys, to Boogie Barnes's flat which he very kindly lent me, but left it a bit of a mess, which made him absolutely furious. He called me a fascist, and I didn't see him again until I was a rather inexperienced, albeit prize-winning, copywriter, and he was at the top of the tree.

29

At RAF Heaton Park in the autumn of 1943 I borrowed a bicycle to run an errand for the orderly room and found, on my return, that I had been riding Group-Captain Tyler's bicycle. I was put on a charge and then confined to camp for a couple of weeks. The punishment was light, but I was not glad to be noticed as the man who had 'stolen' the CO's bike. I knew from conversation with a WAAF who typed his letters, and to whom I had sold a few copies of the *Daily Worker*, that there had been correspondence between him and the RAF police about my former membership of the Communist Party. This, I supposed, was why I had failed to be placed on a draft to Canada or Rhodesia for so long. Everyone with whom I had been posted from Cambridge had already gone and were no doubt now flying more advanced aircraft and eating unrationed food in the sun.

Meanwhile I was getting what I could out of being in Manchester, which included going out with the beautiful Gwen Olinsky, who worked at the communist bookshop in Manchester and lived with her parents at Bowker Vale. I had heard of her at Central Books; Alf Silverman had seen her; Bagenal Harvey talked of her in such a way that she seemed to be a Queen of Sheba of the North. She was not in any way disappointing after all this, but she was as sensible as she was beautiful and did not allow herself to be quite carried away.

Central Books continued to send me cigarettes and encouraging messages, as they had to Ben Zonena before I left – he had joined the army. I drank more tea and Vimto than beer, in fact I don't remember Manchester pubs at all. But I remember being told that the wall round Heaton Park had been built by unemployed mill-workers; I remember the Central Library, and the rain, and the comfortable Jewish families around Blakely, and the way that all doorstep conversations quickly arrived at the point where I was invited to come in and have a cup of tea, love.

It was at Heaton Park that I first met Gideon Cohen. As soon as I heard him speak I heard, in the snow-covered surroundings among the Nissen huts at the lowest part of the park, the warm and familiar accents of Bunce Court. Gideon wore a PALESTINE shoulder flash on his uniform and was a 'mature student' (we didn't use the expression then), aquiline, very cheerful and polite. Since we were talking about the news at the time, possibly about the long-delayed US and British aid to Tito, he may have recognized me as a communist from what I was saying. I was, after all those days and nights in Red Lion Square, a fairly fluent advocate of communist policies.

There was something typical about the way that London communists talked: almost forty years later I was able to identify a friendly Norwich bookseller as an old CP member after hearing him speak a few sentences. We were clear and dogmatic and rather boring, however radical, trenchant and outrageous in our views. We also had a sort of salesman's persistence of tone; even the emotional as distinct from the intellectual communists had it.

Gideon had too much humanity and sense of humour to be impatient with me. He knew better than I did that underneath all the ideology I was young and idealistic and soft, whatever I might pretend. We spent some pleasant mornings reading and talking about all sorts of things over cups of tea in a sort of servicemen's club organized by local citizens. He was studying English literature, which he later taught in Israel, and waiting to be posted somewhere to train as a navigator. This skill and his knowledge of RAF practice and organization he was to use later in one of Israel's wars; but he declined an invitation to take up a military career with the Israeli Government.

I did, eventually, get 'on the boat', as it was called. I sailed with hundreds of others from Liverpool early in 1944 in the *Empress of Japan*, renamed the *Empress of Scotland*. This was a liner that had sailed between San Francisco and Yokohama before the war. Below about 'D' deck the fire instructions were in Japanese.

We zigzagged a great way out into the Atlantic and encountered some rough weather: from my perch at an Oerlikon gun above the bridge I had a marvellous and awful view of the bows and the giant waves. The ship's pitching rhythm and that of the waves were not the same; but when the bows dipped smack into a wave the spray whipped across my face a little while after the great wings opened out below me, and cocoa seemed really something to be grateful for. Below, it was crowded and warm, the atmosphere flavoured with cigarette smoke, sweat and vomit. There was bread of a dazzling whiteness on this ship, and rather more hot-dog sausages than I'd normally wish to see. There were also Hershey Bars and Sweet Caporal cigarettes, known all over Canada as Sweet Caps, in Cellophane, with silver paper – but no cigarette cards.

Much as I wanted to fire my gun, I don't think a single submarine was sighted. We steamed past the rocky, unappetizing Nova Scotia coastline and docked, after about a week at sea. The winter snow had not yet gone.

30

What did I do in Canada? We used to sit on our beds or bunks between courses, in dispersal units or holding camps, or doing odd jobs in other units, and ask each other ironically 'What did you do in the war, Daddy?' – and get answers of varying sarcasm or obscenity or surrealism. In our brief bursts of actual flying we were more cheerful as well as busier, and nearly all conversation was about the behaviour of aircraft or the talk of instructors. I spent about fourteen thousand hours in Canada, and seem to remember from my Pilot's Log Book before I lost it that I flew for just seventy of them.

I went, eventually, to two different Elementary Flying Training Schools, one in Manitoba and one in Yorkton, Saskatchewan, and to one Service Flying Training School in Calgary, Alberta. I flew the Fairchild Cornell, a low-powered, single-engine, low-wing monoplane; the Cessna Crane, twin-engined, with two pilots' seats side by side; and the Harvard. The Harvard was wonderfully noisy: the propellor tips rotated at somewhere near the speed of sound, which accounts for the noise, and they were only nine inches clear of the runway on take-off. Take-off was at ninety miles an hour, the fastest I'd ever been on land.

I was lucky in a way, with Harvards. I played forty-one games of badminton one evening with tall, black Lester Young (who beat me 21–20), in a pair of borrowed gym-shoes. Next day I had a blister, and the next week I was in hospital with some sort of meningitis. Eight weeks later Calgary had switched from Cessna Cranes to Harvards. I'd missed my course, and escaped Bomber Command too – or possibly even the dreaded glider-piloting. I disliked twin-engined aircraft with vibrating tailplanes and no aerobatic capabilities; and I still wanted to 'fight in the air' as they'd said at Halton all those years ago, not drop things on people.

In the event, it was VE day, soon followed by VJ day. We were grounded – someone at Medicine Hat had done silly things in an aeroplane on VE day – and then told that if we wanted to go on flying we'd have to sign on for an extra five years after our release date. Bravely and miserably, most of us said 'Stuff it'. 'I'm going to buy a motor bike,' someone said.

What I really wanted to do in Canada, flying apart, was to travel like W.H. Davies, or like the poor heroes of Dos Passos's *42nd Parallel*, on a freight train. Canada had only two railways, the CNR and the CPR, though you sometimes saw boxcars bearing the name LACKAWANNA, or SANTA FE. But the train whistles sounded the same and the rolling stock was the same as in the USA. Huge trains pulled out of the freight yard in Moncton several times a day, bound for St John, Halifax, Montreal. I struck up an acquaintanceship with a telegraph operator in a railway office in Moncton – it was an all-night job – who gave me a few timetables and let me read his tickertape. He was amused at my ambition and gave me good advice about where and when to 'grab' my first 'handful of boxcars'. The third time I went to St John in this way I got there early on a sunny morning and was told by a rather drunk man leaning against a hut in St John freight yard that it was 'Dee – double – damned – Dominion Day'. So it must have been 1 July 1944.

I made the trip several times, both ways. For the return journey I always used the same train, which started for Moncton after midnight. You could telephone the freight yard and ask: 'What time does four-twelve pull out?' They'd always tell you.

St John, New Brunswick, is built on rock, and has lots of steep hills. The harbour has the greatest rise and fall of tide in the world. In 1944 it had a population of 50,000, so pretty well everyone knew everyone else. Moncton was flat and boring by contrast, and seemed to have no particular reason for being where it was; it might have been built on a landfill site or an old swamp. And St John was a seaport, so people knew there was more to the world than this particular corner of it. It even had a kind of polite society as its top layer, with dock-workers and casuals as its bottom one. When I persuaded Gideon to 'ride the rods' with me – we sang and told stories through the hundred miles or so of forest – we moved in polite St John circles, beginning at a quite posh servicemen's canteen or club, and actually hearing some classical music played at some point. It was really a stroke of fortune that landed us together in Moncton as well as Heaton Park. We had a few friends in common, notably an ex-actor called Penney, a charming and slightly mysterious character, and another wearer of the PALESTINE shoulder flash, David Boyadjian, an Armenian, also from Jerusalem. Gideon showed me his family name on a shop front in the Old City a few years ago; but he is thought to have emigrated to America.

David Boyadjian and I went to SFTS in Calgary together, and he failed the course, which made me feel obscurely guilty for having encouraged his strange way of life, even though it was his flying skill that let him down. He was without doubt the most devoted and obsessive pursuer of women I've ever met. He had black curly hair, wide brown eyes, rather full lips and a most disarming and yet wicked smile. Whenever he saw a woman he fancied, he looked her straight in the face and smiled like a sun-lamp, saying 'What's your beautiful name?' Though most Armenians are Christians, he was like a charming and hospitable sultan inviting girls into the sort of Paradise that good Muslims are promised after a glorious death but which he appeared to be enjoying in advance. With him, I was suddenly aware that the freight train to St John was much less comfortable than hitch-hiking. But when we got there for a week's leave he happily accompanied me to the Longshoremen's Union office, where Leslie Fiedler, looking not unlike the character in *On the Waterfront*, another union boss, found us jobs as trimmers on a coal-boat in the harbour at a dollar and eight cents an hour – two dollars and sixteen cents for night work. Fiedler was not rough-tongued or crooked but on the contrary quietly spoken and even a bit English-sounding. Anyway, labour was short and we were delighted.

We worked in the hold of this ship which was unloading softish coal, possibly for a gasworks, shovelling under the shadow of the grab which took out perhaps a ton at a time, and finally emptying the corners of the hold under the bulkheads. We walked to the hostel we were staying in in all our blackness and showered. The last bit of you from which coal-dust washes is the skin round your eyes; so we had a strange look about us on our way to a meal or a dance. We spat black for days after we'd finished. But we needed the money. Pay in Canada went even less far than pay in England.

31

I'm strongly tempted, in 1992, to get away from Canada and out of the RAF as quickly as possible, but I should be a little grateful to Canada first. It was there, wasting time at another station between courses, at Picton, Ontario, on a peninsula jutting southward into Lake Ontario, that I began to think I might be able to write. Central Books still sent me letters, and I still wrote back. I have a feeling that Sadie, who was a good writer, wrote some of the letters from the bookshop. At all events, while I was at Picton I was sent to a bombing range at RCAF Mountain View, to sit in a small hut high up on a hillside and plot the bomb-bursts – little puffs of white smoke on grass and scrub down in the valley. The rations were excellent and the hut was comfortable. The table was a little like the drawing-board in the architect's office where I'd worked, and I was alone for hours at a time. I wrote letters. I found myself describing the space and the silence, both of them filling me with delight; and the solitude. It would be seven years before I wrote anything I thought worth printing, but this was the first time I wrote anything worth writing.

I had begun to read verse at Picton. I spent a good deal of time with a trainee pilot called Johnny Kearns, and one of us had a copy of Herbert Read's *The Knapsack*, one of the best of all anthologies. I think it belonged to me, but between us it seemed to come to life and increase in value. I don't know why it suddenly became possible to discuss poetry, even to utter it; but whatever the reason, the result was that I began to take possession of what was written, which before had been as far out of my reach as the words round the inside of the dome at the Marsham Street church: AND GOD SHALL WIPE AWAY ALL TEARS FROM THEIR EYES; AND THERE SHALL BE NO MORE DEATH. . . . FOR THE FORMER THINGS ARE PASSED AWAY. I saw that poems had been written by men and women, and could be grasped by men and women. Until then I might have belonged to a different species from the poets, or been a child able to hear adult conversation but not to take part in it.

Johnny and I worked several days and nights in a local cannery, loading a boat with cases of tins of tomatoes. We saw the shore of the lake, with waves like waves of the sea. I don't think he came to Calgary with me.

Calgary was the farthest west I was stationed in Canada, but I had some leave after the meningitis and rode a freight train across the Rockies to Vancouver. It was cold around the Kicking Horse Pass, after Banff, but as the train went down the far side of the mountains it got beautifully warm and rich with deciduous trees and water and places called Salmon Arm, and Golden. 'Golden, BC', you'd write on an envelope. At Revelstoke there was a long wait and I had been given the address of a Mr Petch, a retired railway worker who lived there. He gave me a good meal and told me how to proceed to Vancouver. I was to climb up on to the narrow platform at the front of the first carriage of a passenger train, with a steel bar to hold on to across the blanked-off half of the corridor connection, behind the locomotive tender (never mind the cinders, he said), and at Kamloops jump down on the side of the train away from the platform, run round the rear of the train and get into a coach and go to sleep. If anyone asked me for a ticket, I had given it to the conductor already. 'They change the crew at Kamloops,' said Mr Petch. So that's what I did.

In Vancouver I met Ruth Penner, whom I'd liked so much in Winnipeg. Her father was a communist alderman and she was in the Canadian Women's Army Corps. They wore khaki tunics with brass buttons carrying the head of Athena. She cut one off for me and I kept it a long time. I don't know what went wrong between us; I know we wrote to each other a lot; but I suppose I was not going to stay in Canada and didn't want to marry. It was very sad and sweet and silly; but she was lovely, and only silly as people are when they can't master their feelings.

I'd had a few girl-friends in Canada. Once in St John I'd kissed a black girl on the stairway of the wooden house she lived in with her parents, late at night, both of us terrified; I don't know what of. Her name was Olive, and she had a job setting up pins in a bowling-alley. She wouldn't go anywhere with me; just walk home when she finished work. Her father was a sleeping-car conductor. I don't know whether she could read or write.

Coming back on the *Ile de France* in the autumn of 1945 without zigzagging or manning guns I met Abe Cohen again, looking much less boyish, with a sweat-rag round his neck: he was a ship's cook. I told him what we'd had for pudding. 'Oh,' he said, 'that's Board of Trade duff.'

I had a pair of blue jeans in my kitbag, and two plaid shirts. I'd never seen a lumberjack all the time I was in Canada. I was told I had a discernible Canadian accent even when I wasn't imitating Canadian radio – '*This is CFCN, the friendly voice of the Prairies in Calgary, bringing you the latest hog prices and the voice of – Wilf Carter!*' – and I had been taught in hospital in Calgary to roll cigarettes by a flight mechanic in the RCAF who told me he was a cowboy in Civvy Street.

I also had another eighteen months to spend in uniform.

Part Three

32

By this time we were all a great deal less 'airmanlike' than we'd ever been. Corporal Taffy Baines at 2 ITW had nannied us into a rather smart, even swanky, squad. 'You play the game with me,' he'd announced, 'and I'll play the game with you. You drop in the shit and I'll step on your 'ead and push you under!' But no one was pushing now. We'd missed our wings parades by weeks or months and we'd refused the extra five years; there was nothing now but some more or less despised ground job. So we scrounged and fiddled and left everything unpolished; we were cynical and lazy and thought everything a joke. We lived from leave to leave, including forty-eight-hour passes, and couldn't wait to get into civilian clothes.

Gideon Cohen had probably advised me to go and see my mother when I got back; if he didn't, I'm sure at least that he seriously approved of my expressed intention to do so. He himself had visited Lansdowne Walk to assure her of my survival. I telephoned and then turned up. I presume I made an apology for giving her so much worry for three and a half years. But she had been in touch with Bagenal Harvey, she said, so it had not been quite so awful as I had imagined. She called him Harvey Bagenal and I gave up correcting her after one try; it must have been uncomfortable for her to have had to speak to him on the telephone in the circumstances of 1942. Meeting Bruce and Jeffrey and Sally – who by now was calling herself Sonia, her official name – was much easier. Their pleasure in seeing me was easier to accept than my mother's. And we were all a bit older, and could talk. Sally – Sonia – was charming and sweet, especially when my mother was not around; Jeffrey was between being oppressed by his youthfulness and being liberated by his precocity; but with Bruce I began to spend, in the last months before my release from the RAF, a great deal of time full of learning for me and perhaps for us both.

The most surprising change at Lansdowne Walk was that my mother had let half the house to the Soviet Military Mission – that is, to a couple of officers and two secretaries: Nina Patova and Sasha Yazynina. Bruce and I took them to the big Picasso and Matisse exhibition at the Victoria and Albert Museum on 13 January 1946. Because of my politics I was a bit disappointed and dismissive about the Matisse. Nina and Sasha didn't like Picasso at all; when reminded that he was a communist they just lifted their shoulders and pursed their lips, eyebrows raised. If Picasso was a communist at all, he certainly wasn't a Soviet communist.

At Christmas, Bruce had given Sasha a copy of Dickens's *A Christmas Carol*, and for my twentieth birthday three weeks before that Nina had given me the leather-bound 'Five Year' diary in which I've just checked the date of the V & A visit. By that time Nina and I were on terms of intimacy. We had what is nowadays called fancied each other from our first meeting; we spent hours sitting in the basement kitchen at Lansdowne Walk drinking tea, with and without Sasha, and eating blackcurrant jam out of saucers. Nina was teaching me Russian: some of the diary referred to is written in Cyrillic script to disguise its cruder content. It contains references to long lists of books, films and girlfriends – or of young women I was carrying on or attempting to carry on with.

Incidentally, I find in the diary an explanation for my uncertainty about the meeting with Ruth Penner in Vancouver. 'What went wrong' between us was that I felt I had to tell her, sitting in a Chinese restaurant in Vancouver with the juke-box playing 'Till Then' (Mills Brothers), that on my last night at the EFTS near Winnipeg I'd gone to a dance there and taken a Ukrainian girl I met at the dance to a room in an hotel off the main street and slept with her. I didn't tell Ruth I didn't know the girl's name – we called each other 'you' – or that despite our having satisfied our desire for each other she had been too shy to remove all her clothes. This is only one of several remorseful notes in Nina's diary, and mentions Ruth's tears and my resolve to write to her – I still had her photograph and presumably her tunic button. A few months later Ruth sent me a shirt across the Atlantic and I immediately and happily put it on and continued my social life on leave in London, which included visiting the barber's shop next to Central Books, going to see another woman who said 'next time' – meaning next time I was on leave – and having three friends from Central Books back to Lansdowne Walk, where it seems Bruce and I cooked a 'terrible' supper. This last remark reminds me how young we were: any 'terrible' meal Bruce cooked would have to have been eaten or pushed aside about forty years ago. He just doesn't cook terrible meals. Nor does Jeffrey.

Three days before I received the shirt from Ruth, on 3 August 1946, there is an entry to the effect that Bruce and I took Jeffrey to a meal at Bianchi's in Frith Street and then to Ruh's Café, 'who now knows all 3 of us'. Jeffrey was fourteen at this time, Bruce eighteen, and I twenty.

33

Nina was supposed to come and see the new year in with me at Wigtown, where I was stationed in the late autumn and winter of 1945/6. But at Christmas I went to a party with some Central Books people, with a high temperature due to incipient flu, and ate lots of fried chicken and drank lots of white wine and other things and got jaundice. So I spent the first three weeks of 1946 in hospital in Vincent Square and read *War and Peace* in the first nine days of it, which Nina brought me on New Year's Eve. This was followed by Malraux's *La voie royale* (The Royal Way) and some works of consumer fiction. I spent my twenty-one days' sick-leave in Bagenal's flat in Red Lion Square. Bagenal had flu and was staying at Marie Shapiro's, where the chicken-and-wine party had been held. I spent the first day reading Sherlock Holmes in bed: the short stories are strangely comforting, I find, when I'm ill. I never quite manage to get them by heart, so there's always some uncertainty about what's going to happen, cosily familiar as they are in the main.

As well as the great Picasso exhibition, Bruce and I went to see Epstein's *Jacob and the Angel* in a gutted shop in Oxford Street, its front covered with exclamatory notices: HAVE YOU SEEN . . .? YOU MUST SEE . . .! The great reddish stone sculpture had been bought by some showman as a freak or sensation. I supposed that by now it was more likely to be in some Disneyland than in a tall, cool cathedral, until I was reminded that it is in the Tate Gallery.

On the same leave I saw Harry Smolins and Gwen Olinsky, who were soon to get married. Bruce and I went to a concert with them at the People's Palace and afterwards wandered about the East End eating bagels and drinking coffee. Bagenal and Maja Beuer were going to get married too; they were already living together and were soon to move from Red Lion Square to Maresfield Gardens, where Sigmund Freud had lived. Bagenal left Central Books that year and became something of an entrepreneur, first going into an organization called World Film Publications with Paul Hamlyn, Michael Hamburger's brother, and then becoming an agent for various sportsmen who needed to supplement their incomes by posing for advertising photographs. An early member of his stable was Denis Compton whose picture appeared on Brylcreem posters, though without his name. Bagenal was generous about paying for drinks and meals, and would always lend me money. He employed me once or twice when I needed to make a little money on leave, and even as late as 1952 or 1953 he put me up at a house in Kent which he was doing up and paid me to work in the garden. But the idea of his becoming a businessman made me feel less comfortable with him, and I tended to diverge from him more and more. I suppose that by the time I was thirty we lived so differently that we'd be unlikely to meet: by that time I had lived precariously indeed and was only gradually climbing out of an economic crevasse. In another three years I started work in an advertising agency myself, as a copywriter; but by then we had lost touch.

At Wigtown I had read *Howard's End* in December; by February I had read practically all Forster, including a second reading of *Howard's End*. I had also read George Borrow and Conrad, Lermontov's *A Hero of Our Time*, and an equal amount of fast fiction. The strongest impression of all seems to have been made by Forster's *The Longest Journey*, which I found painful as well as interesting.

After meeting Kenneth Cheeseman again – we ate in Soho and talked far into the evening at the Café Royal – I went back to Red Lion Square and wrote my first story. It was certainly autobiographical and involved a relationship with a young woman, but I remember nothing else about it; only that from this time I began to think of myself as some sort of writer, a very exciting idea for me. I wrote another one at Wigtown in March, and showed it to Harold Alston on a weekend I spent with him and Arthur and Brenda Roberts in Cockermouth. I sent it to *Men Only* where Harold knew a sub-editor, but it came back with a kind and encouraging letter: 'The great thing is to stick at writing and in twelve months you will laugh at this early effort. . . .' I have the letter in front of me: it is written in red ink in a flowing yet quite precise hand, and signed rather oddly 'The Editor'. So I went on reading a great deal and writing little but letters. I began to see how derivative my stories were and often abandoned them in disgust after a couple of paragraphs. Nothing, however, could make me forget the happiness of sitting in my hut at Wigtown with snow on the window and the stove crackling quietly, actually busy about what I knew was my business, whether it failed or succeeded.

34

It is possible that in 1946 I saw more films than in any other year. There were always RAF camp cinemas, and besides them I went to see current films in local towns, such as *Brief Encounter*, which I saw both at Eastchurch on the Isle of Sheppey and at Gloucester, where I worked at RAF Records. On leave in London I saw Carné's *Le jour se lève* no less than five times: instead of saying to each other 'Let's go to a film', Bruce and I used to say 'Let's go and see *Le jour se lève*.' It was on at Studio One, Oxford Street, with Terence Rattigan's comedy, *French without*

Tears. Getting to know the second feature so well was a bit like getting to know a show in the theatre if you were working backstage. It was irritating at first, since suicide and tragedy were what we were there for, but it began to be quite tolerable and amusing. Fortunately it was very well done: Roland Culver was especially good.

Carné was the great thing, though. At the Everyman I also saw *Le quai des brumes* twice that year. *Les enfants du paradis* must have been shown as well by then, or soon after.

I think Bruce and I were equally anxious to go to France, but I had to wait to get out of the RAF and Bruce had to spend some time working out his National Service as a conditionally exempted conscientious objector. He did some time at the West London Hospital for Nervous Diseases, which didn't sound too cheerful, and he was soon sacked because of his 'aristocratic attitude', he said. I began to pick up snatches of Freudian psychology, and heard of electroconvulsive therapy for the first time. ECT sounded utterly terrifying then, and now seems even worse. Sonia my sister underwent it as a non-voluntary patient more than once. But that was after my mother died and Sonia and her husband took over my mother's flat in Earls Court, four years later. A sinister place I thought it.

If ECT sounded frightening, why is there no mention of the two enormous horrors of 1945 – the bombing of Hiroshima and the discovery of the death camps? Speaking out of his feelings at the time, I believe Stephen Spender said that henceforth poetry was impossible, or words to that effect. This was about the bomb. Certainly little was said about it in the RAF: it was perhaps literally unspeakable. The same with Belsen and Buchenwald and Auschwitz. The works of Primo Levi, to take just one instance, were not yet available. There was film, admittedly; but even with the image in front of one's eyes, it was still unimaginable. Only in 1954, at the time of US hydrogen bomb tests in the Pacific, do I remember beginning to realize something of what had happened in Hiroshima and Nagasaki. I believe that the extermination camps took even longer to begin to be real. Until then I think many people fended off thinking about them by thinking instead of the notorious wickedness and evil that Nazism and fascism represented. It was so much easier to blame the guilty than to suffer, even in the imagination, with the victims.

Sitting in Tony's, a Greek Cypriot café in Charlotte Street, during one leave in 1946, I remember Bruce and another man talking about

Dresden, while I somewhat shamefacedly tried to justify the thousand-bomber raids. My opinions wobbled a lot in those days. Bruce's conscientious objections seemed unassailable to me. I knew the Communist Party was liable to be economical with the truth; I had little love or trust for the authorities, wherever they might be; but wrapped up with all I knew was the fear that my idealistic notions about liberty and justice could not be separated from military and political means. I began to be a bit ashamed of my communism, and at the same time ashamed of my disloyalty to it. But Tony's, with or without Bruce, and the Soho pubs from the Duke of York to the York Minster, were my university; and in those days there was the extension provided by Lyons Corner Houses. In the Strand and in Coventry Street and Marble Arch they stayed open all night, and in 1946 I spent many nights in one or another without even using amphetamines to stay awake, having the corners knocked off me and gradually taking up a different position. I won't call it a 'stance', since – about politics at least – I became much more relaxed. I began to be far more interested in trying to become a writer and much less in being a politician. I ceased, except for reading the *Daily Worker* and *Reynolds News*, the last left-wing Sunday paper, to read political material.

And I became fascinated with jazz. On leave in London, in Gloucester, even in Glasgow one day, having to wait for a train, I bought ten-inch records of Bessie Smith, Armstrong, Waller, Bechet, Beiderbecke, Jelly-Roll Morton, Wingy Mannone, Muggsy Spanier, Billie Holliday. In Gloucester I ran a jazz record club with an airman called Frank, a 'discography professor', and another called Dick Sewell. At Pachesham Lodge Bruce and I had already encountered Louis Armstrong, and I had at least heard of Fats Waller, though I thought he was called 'Fat Swallow'. Now I began to collect him; he seemed to offer almost inexhaustible amusement and virtuosity and excitement, as well as applying a refreshing iconoclasm to the sentimental song.

35

The year 1946 was my last whole year in the RAF. I followed two courses: one, to become an air movement assistant (AMA), a trade I never actually took up, and about which I know nothing now except that it was to do with the loading and disposition of freight in transport aircraft and the associated paperwork. The other course was academic and enabled me to sit for the Civil Service Commission Forces' Preliminary Examination, which was regarded as equivalent to Higher Certificate and qualified me for university entrance. I passed it easily and had only to relearn some Latin on my own in order to go to Goldsmiths' College on a degree course for teachers in 1950.

Apart from following these courses, which were short and undemanding, I was employed smashing and/or burning unwanted RAF equipment, guarding German prisoners of war, and as a clerk in RAF Records at Gloucester.

The time left over from these courses and duties, and from my pursuit of literature, films and music, was devoted to a more or less uninterrupted series of sexual and emotional adventures with women, including adultery, fornication, unsuccessful love affairs, betrayals of friends and multiple infidelities. I attended scores of dances, on and off camps, and seem to have paid attention to hundreds of attractive women. I was a most susceptible, naïve, hypocritical and unscrupulous young man. There are 'serious', and even 'remorseful', entries in the diary, but they only throw into sharper relief the details of my attempted and successful affairs and my shameless and on the whole cheerful sexual tourism.

I don't know how to explain this, so I won't try. 'Fear of not flying,' I might say, if a bad joke would meet the situation; or 'being unfaithful to my mother'. If I look at myself now, nearly fifty years on, I still see very recognizable remains of susceptibility and hypocrisy. I'm still easily swayed, if not overcome, by women's niceness and beauty, and I still enjoy talking about the way human beings behave. If I sometimes think I shall be all right when I'm lying decently still and silent in my coffin under the grass of Kenninghall churchyard, it's mainly because I can't really imagine ever being *quite* all right until then.

Studying during leaves in London to be a Bohemian, on the other hand, I was much more innocently employed. Remembering white nights in Lyons Corner Houses or in Covent Garden, and sleeping on chairs or floors in friendly houses or flats, always involved in discussion, and with variously qualified and motivated fellow-students and 'tutors', I remember myself as I am now. I was growing, from being a Bohemian and unpublished writer, into a slightly published, slightly less Bohemian one. It took a very long time.

Three of my first tutors were Wilf, Sammy and Colin. I don't know what their other names were, as we didn't use them then. In the same way people drank together in Soho pubs night after night and told each other quite secret, intimate, personal things, but often didn't know where their friends lived. For many, homes meant constraints on speech and behaviour; in Soho, people relaxed and were either themselves or took up roles they preferred.

I first met those three in the Strand Corner House, though I'd seen Wilf in Tony's or the Duke of York. I had had a busy Sunday going to lunch at Lansdowne Walk, which Sonia cooked in my mother's absence, really beautifully. 'Mother's absence really did wonders for her,' says the diary. 'But she was afraid of her return; there was sure to be a "row" – about anything at all. . . . She was charming and sweet. I went a little while after Bruce and joined the *Maltese Falcon* queue in Edgware Road. Saw him across the road under a shop window awning with a v. dark girl who turned out to be Spanish and laughed immoderately at our conversation before the film. Sydney Greenstreet was great.' That evening I had dinner with Harry and Gwen Smolins and Sidney Mittelman, and Harry's sister. 'She, Mit and I at long last got a taxi to Theobalds Road. They went on and I, after hesitation, went to Lyons Corner House, the Strand.'

I had enough money for scrambled eggs and coffee, and a pot of tea, apparently. Over the tea I met and began talking to a man nursing a cut wrist. He said it had been cut with a broken glass, by a woman. He added that he was protecting his face at the time. Then the faculty drifted in and sat at a nearby table, and I joined them. They were arguing about whether words actually mean anything. In themselves, that is. Is it just an accident that *ball* sounds round, and *bubble* sounds multiple? Onomatopoeia apart. . . . Wilf, black-haired, black-bearded and with wide blue eyes, mainly listened to the argumentative Sammy and thin-lipped, moon-faced, querulous Colin. Sammy had what the diary calls 'a mediocre-ish red beard'. Colin wore a very tired-looking brown suit, a brown pork pie hat, and 'an old greyish shirt with rust stains'.

Wilf began to talk about Berto Pasuks, a black dancer, and about 'Berk, a choreographer'. At this distance in time I can't be sure that he wasn't quietly having everyone on. Anyway the detective with the moustache told us to get out, or move on. Were we laughing too much? I rather think this was a quiet and civilized exchange of ideas, as if we owned the place and had all the time in the world; but possibly Colin had raised his voice. We walked to the Coventry Street Corner House, 'a motley crew, I suppose. Wilf, who wore sandals winter and summer, looked "like Jesus Christ" and the rest of us sang marches and the classics'.

I remember quite a lot of 'singing' of instrumental music in those days. Harry Smolins and I were fond of doing the second movement of Beethoven's Seventh as a duet. Bruce and I got a long way into Schubert's 'Great' C Major Symphony once in the York Minster. 'Excuse me, sir,' said Gaston, 'but we haven't got a licence for singing.'

In Coventry Street Wilf and I saw something extraordinary: a woman with red hair and a blue overall scrubbing, pink-faced, at a large area of fawn tiles. Inside we had some friendly chat with a couple of prostitutes who were having a rest and a cup of tea, and I rolled a great many cigarettes for different people, having shared theirs.

'We left the Corner Ho. at about six and walked to Covent Garden in the dawn. It had rained. Wilf recited a long poem by G.M. Hopkins. We sat in a caff in Bow Street. Wilf ended the argument about words by saying to Colin: "All right, I'll give you a word: OM!"

'"I'm not in tune with it!" cried Colin.

'Coming towards Covent Garden tube station a carter shouted something derisive at Wilf – the market was pretty busy by now – and Wilf surprised me by answering loudly and publicly: "I'll show you some more hair if you like!" The carter backed off looking stricken. Wilf, his eyes dancing, said "I think I must have embarrassed him!"'

36

That was a white night at the end of a forty-eight-hour pass on the way to my second posting to Gloucester from Kirkham, where I'd done the Forces' Preliminary Examination. For the next two months I was occupied in the 'glasshouse' at RAF Records, where one of the civilian women was at first 'very worrying', according to the diary, and then meeting me in Cheltenham for Saturday nights of unmarried bed and breakfast. There was also a WAAF corporal with whom I was besotted, in pay accounts. She married an American. And a Land Army girl, slight and fair, who played darts and drank beer in the Lamb, and had been for long walks with me in June. She was pregnant.

I was really uncertain, after the precautions I'd taken, but I became certain after we'd talked. It must be me. The apple trees between which we airmen hung our washing, next to the huts, and the whole luscious countryside under the August rain seemed to accuse me. I should have to take care of her but I certainly didn't want to marry her. Nor did she want to marry me, she said. Everyone I spoke to said it would be crazy.

The abortion was in London in September. A brisk young woman performed it at an hotel near Russell Square. I'm not going to go through it: what I'll say is that through fear and anxiety I retained my sanity more or less, and that she got through it phlegmatically and uncomplainingly. I hope that in time she got over it too. I think I might have done so if I'd made sure, months or years later, that she was all right. I didn't.

37

Just now I opened the door of the wood stove (this is black spring 1991, the day after the Gulf War) and stuck in some rubbish. Closing the stove door again, I saw yellow flame round the edge. This reminded me of one of my last ambitions.

In the final winter of my degree course at Goldsmiths' (1952–3) I took a job at the Southeast Gas Board's East Greenwich gasworks, in Number Four Retort House – 'the House', we called it. The house! A vast building, something like the exhibition centre at Earls Court, one of four in a row. Railway lines entered the 'houses' half-way up, level with the tops of the banks of retorts. The retorts, long elliptical tubes lined with fire-bricks, were in great blocks about twenty feet high and twenty yards long. Four or five of these blocks went the length of the house; four or five rows of these blocks took up its width. Above was the railway. Trucks discharged slack coal into great pits level with the retorts. Mechanical 'chargers' fed coal into the retorts, like a finger stuffing a pipe with tobacco. After cooking for a few hours, with tubes carrying off gas, tar and ammonia, the coal would be changed into hard coke, bright-red hot, which a hydraulically operated ram would push through the retort. It fell into great chutes with barred grilles at the bottom, not to be released until it had been 'watered down', and until then actually burning. Watering down was done by a man holding a high-pressure hose with a curved, rigid nozzle, who approached the mouth of the chute crouching and with face averted from the blistering heat of the coke, unable to open the valve until the nozzle was over the edge of the chute, and at pains to avoid the explosion of superheated steam which would occur immediately the water came out. This steam from watering down at East Greenwich I saw several times afterwards from Hungerford Bridge, five miles away, beyond St Paul's.

After the coke was out and on to the conveyor, the long tube of the retort, heated by the furnaces below and by the cooking of the coke itself, would glow cherry red inside along all its length. The ones at head height could be seen right through to the small black elliptical door at the other end. The charger would arrive and pump or shove slack coal into the retort, packing it tight like a moulded cigar, and then move on to the next retort. One man of the three-man crew on the charger would catch the cast-iron door of the retort with the end of a steel bar and slam it to. By this time there was an eight-foot plume of flame roaring out of the filled retort. As the door clanged to, the plume of flame would become an oval sunflower with blue petals among the yellow and the door as its centre. The man would reach forward with a gauntleted hand and tighten the door by turning a handle in the middle of it: it was just a door again.

Since I was only a student, and temporary, I did only three different jobs at East Greenwich: watering down, slow firing and hole-clearing. Slow firing meant feeding the furnaces below the retorts with small coke to keep them warm when they weren't in use, or to prepare them for use. Hole-clearing involved standing above the coal-storage bunkers high up in the house while a railway crane with a grab took coal out of them. This happened when stored coal started to smoulder from spontaneous combustion. Come to think of it, I forget what I actually did when I was on hole-clearing. Perhaps I acted as a safety man for the crane-driver. What I do remember is the awful height of the railway and the sullen smoke from the hole.

I loved East Greenwich gasworks. It was Victorian, it was working class – a proper satanic mill. It was also dangerous, so dangerous that the men who worked there were among the cleanest spoken and the most solicitous anywhere I have ever worked. 'Don't get your nose over the hot coke when you turn the water on.' 'Watch how you tread here, it's a bit greasy.'

Walking away from the baths at the end of a shift, pale and clean and warm under a coat and cap in the dark, chill air, I wished the job would go on longer. I wished somebody would ask me, in the avuncular way of older men, 'What's your ambition, son?' 'Shutting doors,' I should have said.

38

Clean spoken those in the RAF had never been, but they struck me as highly articulate, playful, almost surrealistic wielders of language. Not content with their impressive contribution to slang during and before the Second World War, they produced many performers of monologues, who kept alive and handed on an interesting variety of speeches which only needed triggering at the right, or wrong, time and place to be dusted off and trotted out first by one, and eventually, *crescendo*, by everyone in the barrack-room. Some were dialogues but were customarily spoken by one person using two voices. Here's one for silly falsetto and roaring bass:

'Da-ad!'
'WOT?'
'Can I 'ave sixpence?'
'WODGER WANT SIXPENCE FOR?'
'I want ter go ter the Pick-chers!'
'THERE'S PITCHERS ON THE WALL!!'
'Yes, but I want the Moving Pick-chers!'
'I'LL MAKE THE BASTARDS MOVE!!!'

There were pieces that had to be said at speed, if possible all in one breath. You limbered up on this innocent one (time allowed $3\frac{1}{4}$seconds):

’E
sez can you
swim I sez
Oo? ’E sez
You! I sez
Me? ’E sez
Yes! I sez
NAOW!

And when you were ready you performed this one, which is not quite so offensive if you say it quickly:

ACCUSED (*up on a charge of assaulting a taxi-driver*): Well, yer ’onour, it’s like this ’ere. Me an’ the ol’ woman is fuckin’ orf to the pub of a Sat’day night for a bucket o’ mother’s fuckin’ ruin when along comes this ’ere Barstard as calls ’imself a cabby: ’e knocks the old woman a-fuckin’ and a-fartin’ in the gutter. See ’ere, yer barstard, says I, oo d’yer fink yer shovin’ on? Short cock, says ’e. Short cock! says I, so yer missis tells yer everyfink? Arse-oles, says ’e. Arse-oles! says I, I never arst yer where yer come from nor got yer fuckin’ bleedin’ pleasure. An’ with that, yer ’onour, the langwidge as ’ow ’e starts ter use ain’t fit fer fuckin’ bleedin’ publication. An’ I’ll be bitched, bastar’d and bewildered by the ’ole of this fuckin’ court, includin’ yerself in bastard person, if them wasn’t the identical fuckin’ words as ’ow ’e used!

Whom do I see in the barrack-room? Reg Hartlebury, Johnny Kearns, Lester Young, David Boyadjian, a man whose name I forget, one of the best reciters of all, who once called Reg – unless it was Reg who called him – ‘a Middlesbrough-faced twat’, and who said that before he joined he’d been ‘doggin’ up for Accles and Pollock’s’. Legendary stuff.

All the same, I was glad to get out in my cheap demob clothes, with a travel warrant to London and everything to come. I had a ‘Raglan-style’ overcoat, rather thin, in brown herring-bone tweed. It reminded me of Trevor Howard in *Brief Encounter*. I couldn’t wait to swop it for a donkey jacket.

39

Nina went back to the USSR in June 1946. I got cards and letters from her from Holland and Denmark, then nothing. I don't think Stalin persecuted Tartars – Nina was a Tartar with black hair and high cheekbones – but I can imagine that anyone who had spent a few years in England might be regarded with suspicion. To say nothing of the censorship.

I recorded two more Soho visits in Nina's diary. On one of them I spent a whole weekend without going to bed. People were away or busy and I couldn't stay with them, and the servicemen's hostels all said 'BAOR only'. Wilf and I and two other people walked from the Strand Corner House to Hyde Park Corner by way of the Mall and Constitution Hill. We felt under the bronze blanket at the Artillery Memorial to discover whether or not there was a face under it. We floated flaming paper boats on the Serpentine, and climbed on to the Watts statue called Energy, which is no less spooky than the Artillery Memorial. We all slept at Harry Barnes's house, I uneasily in a chair, Wilf and the other two in a bed, and were told that Bruce was in a bed in the next room. Harry Barnes, a painter who also manufactured fakes, and who was bearded and bright-eyed, with a reputation for being a hard nut, woke Bruce up and we all had tea in bowls. We had lunch in Tony's in Charlotte Street and went to the Tate Gallery to see a Maillol and some 'good Rouaults'. An evening in the Duke of York and the Wheatsheaf where we saw Percy Cunningham whom I met on a more than usually fortunate evening in 1941, also in a Corner House, and who was simply kind and witty. We had supper downstairs in Tony's. Bruce sang *Muss i' denn*; Colin sang something bawdy. We played 'spoof' in the Strand Corner House, walked to Fleet Street, met an acrobat and a Benzedrine addict with a grey face, walked to Piccadilly Circus where Colin did *The Observer* crossword in Coventry Street Corner House. Then we walked up through Soho Square towards Tony's again, for breakfast. It was a fine October morning. In Rathbone Place, outside the Philadelphia Restaurant, we were overtaken by a young Scots poet; he looked like a boy, tall, very fair, very thin. He was called Jimmy Singer. He borrowed Colin's walking-stick and drove a cotton reel from the bottom of Charlotte Street half-way to Goodge Street, and then tried on Colin's hat. Next time I met him he had become James Burns Singer the poet, and told me he had written a hundred sonnets 'better than Shakespeare'. 'Burn, Singer, burn; until you burn your tongue,' said Robert MacBryde. But early on the morning of 20 October 1946 I found Burns Singer charming.

In December I had another leave. 'The nights were mostly spent at the Duke of York and Tony's. I saw a great many paintings and drank with lots of painters . . . especially MacBryde and Colquhoun and Minton (a silly but pleasant homosexual). Everyone seems very pleasant indeed, and Dinora says "Hello Oliver".' Dinora was Dinora Mendelson, her father was a dealer, reputedly both rich and mean, but people may have simply liked the idea of a gracious and beautiful young woman with a skinflint father. She was involved at some time about then with a furniture dealer and self-styled cynic called David Singleton, another Soho habitué, who (like the solicitor Eli Hurwitz) was one of the few people who ate off the top of Tony's menu – kebab or chicken – rather than making do with spaghetti most of the time, and occasionally aspiring to moussaka. She later married the racing driver Leslie Marr.

The following weekend, 'I hitched to London on an impulse and arrived after many vicissitudes at Piccadilly Circus, quarter to seven, and went to Bianchi's for spaghetti. Met Harry Diamond on the way to the Duke. Bruce was there, so were the Schnorrer and the Fine Doll. I roasted chestnuts and bought people drinks. Robert MacBryde and Nelson and I went to Tony's and waited and waited. A brawl started over Dinora's alleged insulting some awful tart (who had got three years for slashing someone) and who screamed filth, undressed, tore down the lapels of Bruce's overcoat, pulled my hair, and tried to get at Dinora again. Her girl friend picked up a knife which Bruce tore away from her. She shouted at Harry Barnes, who hit her, saying "You'll get no porter out of me."

'MacBryde and Nelson and Bruce and I went back to Nelson's, who showed us pictures and books and read Ogden Nash very badly. He made tea and, finally, "beds". MacBryde hid behind an enormous mug Nelson had given him his tea in, sang "Lizzie Lindsay" and finally lay beside me under an enormous rug. Nelson kept on giving advice and offering useless aids to greater comfort. Bruce slept soon, not having slept for two days; Robert put his arm round me and became sarcastic when I didn't like it. He sounded like Colquhoun. But we were all the best of friends in the morning and went to Tony's, where Tina was, and talked, mostly about last night's affray. Nelson has given Bruce a mackintosh. B. & I went to 21 Holland Park [the London Musical Club] where we lunched with Mother and Mrs Armstrong and afterwards played with a grotesque nutcracker and walked to Notting Hill Gate and had tea. B. and Mother went to a Bogart film and I went on a tube to Uxbridge and hitched. . . .'

My first impressions of Johnny Minton were certainly influenced by the attitudes of Robert Colquhoun and Robert MacBryde, who unfortunately felt so insecure themselves that they couldn't admire anyone else – except, now I come to think of it, Wyndham Lewis, a wildly disaffected member of an earlier generation, and Jankel Adler, to whom they were close. Also, I was at first deceived by Johnny's clowning into believing he was a clown, and not a sad and serious person beneath the pose. Nelson Pollard lived in Fitzroy Street, in the flat above Peggy Rutherford, a sweet-natured, large-eyed, melancholy lady from Yorkshire, who sold painted furniture at absurdly low prices to Heal's. She employed me for some time to strip chairs, chests of drawers and so on, in her bathroom, using Gedge's Paint Stripper and washing soda, with large quantities of hot water from her gas geyser. Nelson was a printer, offset litho, and could take Soho or leave it, he claimed. He visited the pubs now and then, and could be relied on to buy a drink or two, but was rather a scold. He was an Indian from British Guiana, and spoke with a slight lisp in a rather superior manner. Someone came up to his flat one day to find him spinning or weaving. He looked up and said: 'Gandhi says you must do tings wid your hands, so I'm doin' tings wid my hands.' He got cross with me and a friend once, for giggling at him, and said that we were nothing but 'the débris of the Champs-Élysées', which increased the giggles. But we apologized, once we managed to control ourselves.

MacBryde's singing and dancing were famous. He danced rarely, but sang often. He had a huge repertoire of mostly Scottish songs, and loved singing about women; even more, singing the woman's part:

> There are three bonnie lassies in Bannion,
> And I am the best of them all . . .

He and Colquhoun were 'inseparable' but they were often separated: Colquhoun would infuriate MacBryde by making up to females. He once played an amazing trick on Colquhoun, by sending him a 'fan letter' which asked him to be in the Wheatsheaf at a certain time. MacBryde went along to see if Colquhoun would show up, which he did. The letter was signed 'Ophelia Bumme'.

Spoof is a game between two players, each of whom holds three matches behind his back or in a pocket, and then brings out in one closed fist as many matches as he chooses. When both fists are out, A guesses how many matches there are in A's and B's fists combined; then B guesses, using A's guess to help him get closer to the truth. The players take it in turns to have the disadvantage of making the first guess. New players find the game 'very psychological'. Julian Maclaren-Ross was an addict, and played for drinks in the Wheatsheaf with some success in the fifties.

Tina was a friendly, cheerful waitress in Tony's café in Charlotte Street who treated everyone – unless they were hopelessly drunk or rude – with familiarity and kindness. About George Kyriakou, whose place it was, and about his friend Takkis, there was always something a little sinister. The café changed hands once or twice owing to George's love of gambling. Tina's simplicity was in striking contrast to this rather gangsterish background. The first time I went in to Tony's after a year or two in France and Corsica, Tina came up to the table and said, strangely: 'And what can I get you, Oliver, my Dear?' That was the first I'd heard of Alec Guinness's role in the film *Oliver Twist*. I think it was Nina who began calling Eli 'Mr Hayley' because she failed to recognize Eli as a first name.

The 'Benzedrine addict' we met in fleet Street was Napper Dean Paul, a mildly pleasant man whose sister, Brenda Dean Paul, used to appear fairly regularly in the tabloid press as a somewhat scandalous member of upper-class Bohemia, the 'Chelsea set' or some such nonsense. I never saw her.

40

When I won the Gold Medal of the Poetry Society for verse speaking in June 1982 my daughter Emma, who had come along to hear me and to see whether I'd succeed or not, took one look at the medal and said:

'Oh, Dad! You've got a medal for being an adult! Well done!'

It's about the size and weight of a petrol cap, and the largest words on it are ADULT GOLD MEDAL. It's being redesigned now, I'm glad to say.

I hadn't intended to be quite so chronological in the foregoing pages; but now that I'm twenty-one in the story, I invoke Henry Miller: *Black Spring*. I read it in Paris in 1948. I was twenty-two, and about to be offered the choice between teaching conversational English in a *collège* in Brittany or in Corsica. Nothing was further from my mind at the time. Paris was cold and bitter in March. The coffee was burnt barley and bread was rationed. At the Mairie du Sixième you could get 'tickets', really little stamps, for bread: *la moitié d'une baguette s'il vous plaît, madame*. And they said PAIN PAIN PAIN and so on, a whole sheet of them.

I had one or two private pupils, and on Wednesdays I went to teach two little girls in the parlour of the convent in the rue de Vaugirard which belonged to the Sisters of St Vincent de Paul. They were wonderfully kind, and gave me soup with beans in it before I started, and precious little money when I left – I used almost to run to the Café du Dôme with it and buy Pernods standing up at the bar, which was cheaper than sitting at a table. The Sisters were poor and their little girls were even poorer; I had nothing at all to complain about. I used to think how nice they were to me, a non-Catholic sinner, who was probably sinning this very minute, et cetera; but I knew nothing about the matter, of course. Pierre Voné, the antique dealer whom everyone called Chérif, had told me about the two Sisters of Charity who looked after him during the Occupation, feeding him and even washing him. When he told them he wasn't a believer so why should they bother, they told him to shut up and continued their ministrations until he was better. I didn't understand. Anyway I don't believe I thought much about sin between ringing the bell at the door in the rue de Vaugirard at 6:30 p.m. and hurrying up the boulevard Raspail to the Dôme at five past eight.

I 'invoke Henry Miller' in the rather grandiose phrase because somewhere in *Black Spring* he says: *I write from scratch every morning*. He is liable to be crossing a bridge over the Seine on a bicycle and at the same time thinking about Brooklyn when he was a kid. He is on his way to see an expressionist painter as a matter of fact, who is throwing a party in the suburbs; but then someone passes in a car and waves and stops.

He changes his mind. Champagne appears. Why is America damned or doomed or whatever it is? Must go and see X, at the *Tribune*: he knows all about cooking mussels. . . .

I like this freedom, though Henry Miller may be more of a fictional character in his Paris books than I want to be. My brother Jeffrey really does write from scratch every week and is not fictional at all, in spite of what the new barman at the Apollo Theatre said when Jeffrey claimed to be himself and was told that there was no such person, it was just the name of the character the play was about. Jeffrey writes from *scratch* – a good name for his flat perhaps, if it didn't already have a number – with the same magical effect as that of striking a light. His face suddenly appears as faces appear on the ghost train: he's a scream.

No, but I wish this were as short as a Low Life column, and half as amusing. Meanwhile, I'm going to have a little freedom with time, as Henry Miller did.

41

19 August 1991. I drive north through Watton and Swaffham and Fakenham to Wighton, where Pippa King is going to paint my portrait. I'm glad when she decides to do it in the kitchen; the glare of light in the conservatory is such that I have a fog in front of my eyes, the mist arising from the cataracts. In the kitchen she gives me an Edwardian folding chair to sit on, and another chair for my feet; an enormous cup of tea, almost a chamber-pot; and I can smoke while she works, and read her bits of Elspeth Barker's *O Caledonia* to keep her amused. I don't think any reviewer has yet done justice to Elspeth's *muckle wit*, and I hope she's well into another novel.

Pippa painting looks different from her social self. Instead of fun and benevolence and slipping past the questions posed by life in its awfulness, her regard is straight, unsmiling, observant, indeed voracious: she drinks vision remorselessly, her eyes darken and change shape, becoming holes in a formidable mask. At incredible speed she has finished the first version. Her daughter Caragh says: 'His eyes are really more . . . petite.' We all laugh. Pippa cheerfully alters them.

I am invited to have a look, and find myself pale and pastel-coloured, almost luminous, instead of black, brooding and radical. There is no doubt, however, that this is myself in spectacles and Emma's blue denim shirt, today and not yesterday. What is difficult to believe is the distance between this and my inaccuracy of self-imagining.

I remember Irving Davis the bookseller sitting in his rocking-chair in the flat at the top of 12 Brunswick Square (the same house I had liked so much during the war, when he was somewhere in the country and his daughter had the flat), looking gnomelike, hook-nosed and cheerfully gloomy, and telling me that he always thought of himself as about twenty years old, with lots of fair hair and very blue eyes. He was a learned person, nearer seventy than sixty when I first knew him in 1955 or so, and he spent much of his time in Spanish monasteries and among Italian book-dealers, buying books which he sold, often to Americans, from his office in Orme Square, and complaining that he hadn't had a holiday for ages. Near Orme Square, in Moscow Road, was, he claimed, 'the gloomiest pub in London', which he used fairly regularly, and with obvious pleasure. He was a marvellous cook and a marvellous host. He delighted in the company of beautiful young women, of whom he knew a great many. Indeed it was a beautiful young woman who first introduced me to him: a dancer.

I first met Beryl Kaye on the stage of the Fortune Theatre. The show was called *Joyce Grenfell Requests the Pleasure*, not a very alluring title, but it ran for more than a year before transferring to New York. By that time I was friends with Joyce herself, and friends with the other two dancers, Paddy Stone and Irving Davies (a young Welsh singer-dancer). They and Beryl had worked on *Finian's Rainbow* and they called her Elder-Berry, or just Elder. She was a very compelling performer and had a strong and rather thrilling speaking voice.

I was employed by the Fortune as an extra electrician; the show had hundreds of lighting cues and needed two extra dimmer boards. In the daytime, three days a week, I did accounts, or rather sent out bills, for a small firm of shirtmakers in Rathbone Place, making extravagantly elegant pound signs at the bottom of the retailers' monthly statements. During the show most of the stage-hands had time for a drink or two between cues. I used to go to the Falstaff. There was a man called George on the tabs: he used to arrive every evening and say 'Ring up! I'm 'ere!'

Joyce was the first of the performers whom I met. I was on tea-drinking and literary terms with her before I even dared speak to

'Elder'. I found Joyce more amusing and sympathetic than I had expected from rehearsals, though I remember her bringing round a box of chocolates for the stage staff just before the dress rehearsal, giving everyone a big generous smile and saying, to those unshaven, beer-swilling, merciless amateur critics, 'Sweets to the sweet!'

She shocked us by claiming that she really enjoyed matinées and liked matinée audiences. Coachloads of WI ladies and schoolchildren was how we saw them. And she was always nice, which we weren't used to. She had no satire, only gentle irony and a sort of kindly mockingness. She was never cruel, though her imitations were pretty accurate. She could nearly do 'Mittel-Europeans', but they weren't quite right so they had to have lisps as well as accents. Her shopgirls were excellent, whether they were selling interior decoration in Bruton Street for fun or face flannels in Boots for a living.

Richard Addinsell, still good news commercially fifteen years after the Warsaw Concerto, was a great buddy of Joyce's and set to music a lot of her lyrics, sentimental and yet sensitive and not without pathos. Victor Stiebel designed her gowns, as they were called. We all had dinner once. I became aware of a subculture, plush rather than posh, of Empire furniture, green velvet, iced soup and slightly naughty prints in exquisite frames. No dust.

Joyce herself was much more posh than plush. She gave me cherries and strawberries and cream at teatime in her King's Road kitchen. She liked blue-and-white crockery and a good cup of tea. She asked me to type out and comment on her verse. She had been a friend of my mother's, and a fellow Christian Scientist, which I think she remained. She adored her husband Reggie, whom I suspected of being a merchant banker but who was extremely pleasant, and she 'loved' her accompanist Bill Blezard. She played me her records of the Ricercare, and taught me the most charming and absurd of French *fin-de-siècle* songs:

Dans le printemps de mes années
Je meurs, victime de l'amour,
Semblable à ces roses d'un jour
Que le même jour voit fanées.

Ah! Gardez-vous de me guérir!
J'aime mon mal, j'en veux mourir!

This unlikely acquaintance and friendship began early on in the run of the show. With a confidence that was new to me, I thought I understood something about Joyce's kindness and sense of humour, and her wonderful combination of *grande dame* and Aunt Sally, and addressed to her a few lines of verse, discussing the impossibility of conversation except between equals, and suggesting:

Say I'm a donkey; and say You're a Horse.

She had a funny number in the show about free-expression dance which contained the phrase 'You're a horse!' repeated several times by the enthusiastic teacher.

So we had tea several times, and I lent her a few poems which she took to Walter de la Mare, who said they were 'real poems' and asked us both to come to tea. 'WJ' appeared in the sitting-room of his grace-and-favour flat in Twickenham in a dressing-gown, neckerchief, shirt and slippers all of different shades of blue. He seemed to me to be in fear of death; in fact he had less than two years to live. His evident frailty may have made me imagine his fear. But he gave renderings of several music-hall songs; in fact Joyce and he swopped songs for a while over tea. Outside was the greatest of plane trees, like a cathedral organ, and below it a stone greyhound or lurcher. It's the one I think of when I tell people that my favourite kind of dog is made of stone, though I don't mind bronze ones.

42

When I told Joyce about Beryl, or rather about my feelings about Beryl, we were sitting in Joyce's sage-green Ford Zephyr in Ladbroke Road late at night. She may have thought that I was trying to communicate some feeling about herself at first – I was tongue-tied about it. But finally she laughed with relief and said I could but try – words to that effect. She told me it was Beryl's birthday on 11 August. I wrote to her and gave her the letter in the theatre. She met me for a cup of tea a day or two later; then I borrowed ten shillings from Michael White, a copywriter from Kenya, and took her to tea at the Ritz.

Beryl's skill and dedication and great attractiveness and energy affected me very strongly and for a long time, in spite of my growing preoccupation with the mysteries of writing, as they appeared to me. Notwithstanding the failure of my first marriage, I seriously contemplated spending the rest of my life with her. My ideas about love, however, were hopelessly tangled and obscure: I couldn't see that courtly love, so clearly described by C.S. Lewis in *The Allegory of Love*, which I used at Goldsmiths' in the study of Chaucer's *Troilus and Criseyde*, was after all only a literary convention. I could laugh at the lines given to George Sanders in the film *The Moon and Sixpence*, when as an urbanely English Paul Gauguin, stricken with leprosy, he leans tragically on the doorpost of his grass- or leaf-thatched hut in Tahiti and says: 'Women are funny little creatures. You can beat them till your arm aches, and they still come back to you.' But I really did think that women were so strangely different from men as to have to be regarded as a different race of beings, a great deal more different from myself than a male of any other colour or culture, and both more holy and more terrifying, deep down, even if sometimes kinder and more sensible in my practical experience.

How could these things be? Quite easily, I think. I had learnt as a little boy from my mother that women were beautiful and powerful and unpredictable, and perhaps unexplainable. Why else should my mother have alternated between intense affection and a kind of fury? Why, when I brought her a little bunch of flowers at the age of three or four, should she have laughed at me and teased me about it before other adults? Why should she so often have asked me, in her odd theatrical way, so that I knew she wasn't being herself, 'Do you love me darling?' (Do you LOHVE meh?) What was the reason for the difference between her musical and prolonged laughter downstairs during an evening party and the severity of her 'Go to your room!'? At Lansdowne Walk I had seen her scrub the kitchen floor with a thoroughness and energy of which no servant would have been capable, and then listened to her account of a court appearance she had had to make because she had been summoned for contempt for non-payment of a bill under a court order: 'Please make that *utter* contempt,' she had said. Even as *esprit de l'escalier* it would have been a bit strong; but I really believe she said it, and felt sorry for the magistrate. At school I had fluctuated between pride in her appearance and her wonderful singing voice, and mortification about her difference from other people's mothers. I was always afraid she was going to say something very loud and clear which would have exposed her and me to ridicule. In fact, I admired my mother but didn't trust her, even at the best of times. At the worst she was capable of exploding into nightmare. Nanny Boys, and another nanny called Christine Chandler, were beautiful and good, especially good, loving and reliable and sweet-tempered; but they were of a lower social class, of course. In some peculiar way they didn't count, even if they were undeniably, luckily, there.

As for Betty Macpherson and Bunce Court, I suppose they came too late to alter my underlying attitudes. Sally and her friends were very much preoccupied with 'beauty' (beauty products and hairdos and fashion at first, and then stardom, an imaginary status remotely connected with acting, if only we'd known it at the time).

I was poorly placed to understand anything about love, even at thirty. I was like one of those hard-bitten 'serving airmen' I used to meet in the RAF, who had done their time in a wide variety of countries in both hemispheres and were still at the primitive stage of thinking that wogs begin at Calais.

43

I sold all my jazz records and all my books except for a Nonesuch Blake, and went to France towards the autumn of 1947 wearing sandals and an American jacket with lots of pockets and a draw-string round the waist, a good rucksack and several pounds of coffee. I followed the advice of Ray Cortens about the clothes, and of another man about the coffee, but unlike the second adviser I didn't get involved with drugs or gold bars. Not long after I was more or less settled in Paris I came across his girl-friend who was trying to get permission to visit him in the Santé prison.

Ray Cortens was a Canadian a few years older than I. I had met him in a Covent Garden all-night café while on leave, and had drawn closer to him in Soho in the summer of 1947. He had a young wife with red hair called Katie, and she or they put me up while I was doing a labouring job on the foundations of the *Morning Star*, then the *Daily Worker*, building in Farringdon Road. I wore boots and no socks, and doused my feet with surgical spirit to harden them. I still got blisters. Ray did no labouring, in fact I'm not sure how he obtained any money at all. Katie probably had a job. Ray was a very cheerful borrower of small sums of money and a grateful recipient of drinks. In any case he lived on extremely little and could sleep anywhere. Unruffled by hardship, he observed life in Soho and in the world generally with great pleasure, and did not, I think, plan very much further ahead than a day or two, or worry at all unless it was about the nature of reality or the existence of God. He was something like a hippie before his time, always smiling and gentle. Some people found this irritating. Once in the Duke of York an extremely dangerous man challenged him to *come outside* (that's how people used to challenge each other to fights), at which Ray stopped smiling and said very earnestly: 'I don't want to come outside with you.' When the tall, fair, hard man asked why, Ray said: 'Because you might hurt me and I don't want to get hurt.' Disbelief and disgust spread over the features of the other, and he moved away.

Ray and I spent hours together, talking about life rather than literature. His literary tastes were odd: the only people I remember his being really enthusiastic about were Thomas Wolfe and George Sylvester Viereck, both writers of very long and digressive works. I don't think he liked precision, though he liked the gnomic nature of some of Blake's writings. The classic moment of the day for being in Ray's company was the one early in the evening when he'd look straight at me through his narrowed smiling eyes in the thin, bearded face – never newly washed or rosy – and say: 'Come on, Oliver, let's go to the Duke (Wheatsheaf, Black Horse, etc.) and see if we can find anybody inneresting or beaudiful, eh?'

In some respects Paris was like an expanded version of Soho, or rather the Left Bank was, but with many more drinking places, with cheap hotels and restaurants, and with the market in the rue de Buci if you were housekeeping. I began in a fairly miserable room near Sèvres Babylone, in the rue Dupin. Chérif or perhaps one of his girl lodgers, Ginou or Papou, then told me about the Hôtel Vavin, next to the Métro station near the Balzac statue, where I got an exceedingly cheap – and very small – room for a month or two. Finally an American sculpture student on the GI Bill, who studied with Zadkine, told me there was a cheap attic room going in his hotel, the Carlton-Palace. He himself lived on the first floor. He was a friend of Bruce's. Bruce had found somewhere to live in the vicinity of the Champs-Élysées, where there were a great many American students and tourists.

Bruce and I saw a lot of each other both before I went to Paris and for a good while after we had returned to England. In Paris about Christmas time we received a visit from my mother, who brought us blankets, I think, with the same name-tapes she had had sewn on them for some boarding-school before the war. They were of good quality, and mine went the way of my rucksack and coffee and practically everything except what I stood up in; but not before the worst of the winter was over. The name of the sculpture student was Jack Crummey. He was thin and blue-eyed and young-looking, even earnest. He said his folks in Boston were 'lace-curtain Irish'. He harboured some very polite, and perhaps a bit repressed, homosexual affection for both Bruce and myself; but he was very honest and matter-of-fact about it and about our unavailability.

Even when Anna Grice, who later became my brother Jeffrey's first wife, came and spent a week or two with me under the lead roof and the skylight, Jack went on being drily humorous and friendly and sharing his *pinard* with us in the evening. He was carving ebony about then, and I took a dislike to the wood for some reason. Anna was very pleasant to wander about Paris with, and cooked very good stews based on *boudin* or blood sausage on the little alcohol stove I used for coffee-making. Yet for all her affectionate behaviour and her gaiety she was not a happy person, and when she drank she became first manic and then depressed and tearful. I don't blame her for the drink; she had had a pretty rough time before she arrived in Soho. The wonder was that she was as sweet as she was, I think.

Bruce and I had at least two important friends in Paris apart from Jack Crummey and Chérif. They were both poets and did not know each other, as far as I remember. One was Kateb Yacine, a very proud and elegant young Algerian who later had some success as a playwright. He was fond of the slightly superior Coupole rather than the slightly sleazy Dôme, and of eating ice-cream. He, Bruce and I exchanged the most frightful obscenities in English and Arabic, which had to be learnt by heart. He had a sort of joke-poem in which we delighted:

Je passe tous les soirs
Dans l'ombre
Devant ta chambre

Dans l'espoir
De te voir
Mais je ne vois
Que la poubelle.

And he recommended us, with plenty of warnings, to a certain M. Zuorro (Danton 35–97) who 'interested himself in young people' and actually gave me some quite impossible translation job concerning economic forecasting – English into French, as I remember it. Absurd. But I suppose I got a thousand or two (old) francs out of it, and a couple of drinks, perhaps even a meal.

The other poet was a Breton, Jean Manach, a ferocious drinker of red wine, gaunt and wild in a seedy overcoat and a collarless shirt. We may have met him in the Foyer des Artistes in the boulevard du Montparnasse, but wherever it was, he was friendly and excited and not averse to speaking his poetry, having another drink, and asking about our lives and views. He seemed to me cheerfully desperate and limitlessly generous-spirited. One night we walked with him somewhat unsteadily back to his small flat up a long, narrow stairway somewhere near Notre Dame, where his wife or mistress cooked us wonderful mussels followed by steak – a feast – and we continued to drink wine. I can almost remember two of his poems: one a sort of dream about escaping from paradise which had become very boring and oppressive, where

Faut pas pisser dans le bassin,
Faut pas piquer les clopes . . .

and another one, world-weary:

Je n'irai plus courir les filles
Car les filles sont trop courues;
Je n'irai plus courir les filles
Car les filles ont trop couru.
Les filles ont couru partout
Et bazardé leurs pacotilles . . .
Je n'irai plus courir les filles.

I've just remembered the end of the first one, which begins: *J'ai fait le mur du Paradis*. It ends:

J'ai fait le mur du Paradis
Et je suis allé boire au Dôme
Là, Dieu, bien fait de sa personne,
M'a servi un apéritif
Sans croire à Son Eternité . . .

Bruce and I stood in front of Notre Dame and walked backwards for the fearful pleasure of seeing the façade apparently closing down on us like the lid of a huge box, and paid our usual visit to Rodin's *Burghers of Calais* on the south side of the forecourt.

To me the most extraordinary thing we did in France was to meet, on Bruce's day off from driving horses for a farmer in the locality, in front of Chartres Cathedral, which I'd never seen, at about lunch-time one Saturday. Even more extraordinary, we seem to have been the only people there.

44

A former accompanist of my mother's, a New Zealander called Trevor Fisher (he later taught me with greater success what was meant by sonata form than he had managed to teach me the piano at Lansdowne Walk), gave me an introduction to the Bodecks in Paris. Harry Bodeck was an old Viennese poet with whom Trevor had become acquainted during his youthful studies, and he lived with his French wife near the Métro station Péreire in the 17th arrondissement. Their flat was very clean and, as it were, frozen – set in its ways perhaps, certainly not in the least Bohemian. They both looked as if they'd had a hard Occupation and were having a tough post-war year or two. They were, however, very kind and gave me a meal once a week, which I needed. They put me on to a couple of private pupils and were delighted when I was offered an assistant's post in Corsica. Mme Imbert-Bodeck gave me two shirts and some voluminous underpants made of fine cotton for which, she said, Harry had no further use. I was in danger of arriving to take up my duties at the Collège Clémenceau in Sartène looking as much of a tramp – or an escaped German prisoner of war – as I had on my difficult trip to Marseille not long before.

Boris, a more or less permanent fixture at the Dôme, a bearded and scrofulous Russian, had urged me to visit the Comtesse Pastrée, who would be delighted if I told her that I admired Lanza del Vasto and had read his *Pèlerinage aux sources*, and would probably make much of me. It seemed just about crazy enough to be worth trying and I set off, hitch-hiking from the Porte d'Italie. It was very difficult and very slow. I got short lifts in, for example, vegetable lorries. I did a great deal of walking and very little eating. At one place I pulled carrots in a field to eat. When, having managed to get to Marseille from Montélimar in one miraculous hop, I went into a bar near the Canebière, I was approached by a cunning-looking fellow who asked me if I wanted to go to Spain. 'Not exactly,' I told him; I was on my way to see a patron a few miles away. 'But surely', he said, 'you're a German.' I said no, I was English, I had a British passport. 'Passport!' said he. '*Everyone* has a British passport!' I realized slowly that I was in a rather awkward position. I had stumbled into a sort of Nazi bolt-hole. I agreed to meet the 'Captain' next day, and withdrew. I went to sleep at the railway station among the Arabs on the station benches: we were all thrown out at about 3 a.m. Then I walked the streets. That was quite interesting too. First, I was stopped by two policemen and had my British passport inspected by one of them while the other kept a tommy-gun pressed into my stomach and I held my hands in the air; then I walked on for a bit and only stopped when, rounding a corner, I saw the biggest rat I've ever seen, sitting on its haunches at the mouth of a street drain, eating something in its forepaws. What really shook me was that, when I stopped, it looked up at me, and then went back to its meal as if it had decided that I represented no danger.

I saw the Comtesse, who had me brought the most beautiful meal of potatoes and salad and a fried egg in its own little metal pan, and butter and bread and a small bunch of grapes. But I couldn't really carry off the pretence that Boris had worked out for me, and simply asked her for the return fare to Paris. Which she gave me. Lanza del Vasto would have to wait; so would the 'Captain'.

The way I got the job in Corsica was that a rather respectable English girl whose name I have forgotten, but who only ever told me her surname, so that I think of her as Miss X to this day, had asked me, through another woman, a strange favour while I was still at the Hôtel Vavin. She wanted to be rid of her virginity. A couple of months later I received by the same intermediary a message to the effect that I must without delay get in touch with a M. Renard at the Office Nationale des

Universités et des Lycées and apply for an assistant's post.

M. Renard was kind and polite and ignored my threadbare appearance. He said that as it was rather late in the year, all he could offer me was a post in either Brittany or Corsica. He even advanced me the fare.

45

In the high beech forest near Vizzavona, half-way from Bastia to Ajaccio, next to the single-track railway through the mountains, wild cyclamen were in flower: thousands of little candle flames of tender pink. Young men in the train, noisily happy to be back in Corsica, shouted 'O! la bella bionda!' when they saw a young woman at a crossing. They sang:

Eramu tre surelli O Frideri
Tutti tre da marita
Cu la sua bella barca
La piu bella sine va
Frideri-i-e

Travelling fourth class on the deck of the *Cyrnos* from Marseille had been a bit chilly, though apparently being followed across the Mediterranean by the planet Jupiter, almost as bright as a moon, was exciting. But in Corsica the smell of the *maquis* and the warmth of the April sun, half-way between Paris and the Sahara Desert, were intoxicating. Cigarettes and drinks were even cheaper than in Paris: the cigarette packets were stamped *Vente en Corse*. Ajaccio at siesta-time was sleepy and warmer still, with palm trees in the streets. The *car* to Sartène, a battered noisy single-decker bus, roared and shuddered and klaxoned round a hundred hairpin bends ascending and descending the intervening mountain ranges, stopped for drinks at Petreto-Bicthisano, skirted the sea at the back of the Golfe de Valinco near Propriano, and arrived, after a final steep climb, in the Place, the main square of Sartène, outside the Café Cyrnos. *Cyrnos*, the name of the steamer on which I'd crossed from Marseille to Bastia, and of the café in which I worked for eleven or twelve weeks that first time in Corsica, is an old name for Corsica itself, as Mona is for Anglesey. Lemprière's *Classical Dictionary* gives it as 'Cyrnus – An island off the coast of Liguria, the same as Corsica; and called after Cyrnus the son of Hercules.' It is mentioned in Virgil's 'Eclogues' and in Pausanias.

I was happier in that café, scribbling away on a marble-topped table and being brought cups of coffee all day long by Emile the waiter, than I had been for a long time. It was a meridional version of my midnights in Wigtown in the hut, with snow on the window and coke in the stove. I'm glad it wasn't one of the hundreds of Café Bonaparte/Bar Napoléon places on the island. I prefer Pasquale de Paoli to the self-crowned Emperor – even Pozzo di Borgo who built a house, overlooking Napoleon's birthplace, of stones taken from the Tuileries. Certain Corsicans still sing a grotesque hymn called 'l'Ajaccienne' whose refrain, *Une autre fois Dieu se fit homme!/Napoléon! Napoléon!*, surely goes beyond adulation into horrid idolatry. Anyway Bruce and I exchanged letters containing a lot of references to the Corsican Ogre; one of the teachers at the Collège repeated the story of Napoleon's mother who, when brought the news of yet another victory, simply shook her head and said, '*Pourrrvou que ca dourre!*' (So long as it lasts!); and I soon found that there was a great deal more to Corsica than that particular cult.

The principal was a most obliging person, almost embarrassingly so: the more outspoken members of staff called him Basile, from some character in Molière. I have nothing to reproach him with, myself. He worked out an absurdly convenient timetable for me which concentrated my so-called teaching hours – all twelve of them – into the space of two days. This meant I had five days a week off, and could spend them as I liked. The sea was rather a long way away, though it was part of the view from the courtyard of the Collège; when I felt like exercise I went for walks in the mountains. At first I was very short of money, having to pay back the fare out of a very small salary, but as soon as I was able to I began to take my food *en pension* in a little restaurant. This was a great improvement on the Collège housekeeper's everlasting beans.

A month or so after I got there, Lucien Marchand, the English teacher, married a local young woman, Rosette Nicolai. Lucien at that time was a serious young man who had suffered a good deal doing forced labour for the Germans during the Occupation. He spoke English with a Scottish accent, having done his year abroad in Coatbridge, Lanarkshire. He loved ships and collected British stamps. He lent me all his books in English, and took me for trips in his new grey 2CV, which coped excellently with the mountain roads.

The wedding was a wonderful affair: the church ceremony was followed by a civil one at the Mairie, and from there to the Nicolai house a huge procession followed the bride and groom. First, all the men; next, all the women; and finally, all the children. People who were invited followed Lucien and Rosette up the stairs of the house and then kissed them both before going in. The children stayed below and were thrown sweets and wrapped-up coins. I found the large numbers of people in the small space overwhelming, and decided to disappear up the road towards Foce. I picked them an enormous bunch of wild cyclamen, which I enjoyed very much. I hope it didn't infringe some ancient custom. But they seemed touched and pleased.

M. Nicolai had an ironmonger's shop in a shady street near the fountain, where women got their water, a few doors past the *pharmacie*. He was a large and kindly man whom I trusted as soon as I met him. He had two other daughters, the most charming young ladies in Sartène, I thought. I was always grateful to Jeannette particularly for inviting me to join her and some other people in the evening promenade before dinner, which was a feature of social life in Sartène. People walked once or twice the whole length of the main street from the Place to the Hôtel Sampiero and back. On nights when the sirocco blew from Africa, there was an after-dinner promenade too. In fact it went on very late because people could not sleep with the strangeness and irritation the sirocco brought. Jeannette spoke not only kindly but wittily; she didn't make me feel strange as the only Englishman in south-west Corsica, or as the strangely important 'Professeur' from abroad. She just talked, with a tendency to find things amusing or make them so. Her sister Mimi I saw very rarely. She had a most beautiful voice with a sort of gurgle in it that you find with blackbirds and nightingales. She was as dark as Jeannette was fair. Rosette was a sort of combination of the two of them, but possibly shyer than either, although perfectly competent as an *institutrice* at the local École Maternelle – a sort of playschool where children could go as soon as they were dry, and which they loved.

Lucien and Rosette are still friends of mine. They live in Paris, where Lucien was principal of a *lycée* in the 5th arrondissement. He knows as much about Paris as he used to know about Corsica, if not more. For the first year or so of our acquaintance I didn't realize that he had a deep sense of humour – we spent a lot of time being polite.

46

Humourlessly myself, I tended to regard all sorts of civilities in Sartène, and sometimes even invitations to dinner, as unnecessary distractions. I had a feeling that what I wrote at the café table was the most urgent task I had. Even English conversation, as it was called, with boys and girls from eleven to eighteen, seemed an intrusion. Not that I thought I was writing anything at all remarkable: in fact I was doing that most necessary thing, getting rid of large quantities of rubbish and learning to write.

I did, however, make a few friends. Dr Benedetti, whose much younger and indeed rather pretty wife ran the *pharmacie* near the fountain, used to take me to outlying villages where he had patients to see. Once we drove ten or fifteen kilometres and were met on the road with mules to finish the journey up a steep and rock-strewn track to a tiny village where the stone houses all had outside staircases, and we were given glasses containing preserved plums in a sort of liqueur. The liqueur was sweetish and insipid: the plum was fiery and well over proof.

On my second visit to Corsica I met some extraordinary people, but that came later. The end of the school year 1947–8 was officially 14 July. Jack Crummey, with whom I had corresponded, said he wanted to take a holiday in Corsica. Everyone at the Collège said Porto was the place, if a beautiful place was what you wanted. Jack arrived in Sartène in June and took a room at the magnificently named but shabby Hôtel César et de l'Univers. He was rather depressed and thinking of chucking Paris and returning to the USA to teach. When term ended early in July, we set off up the coast past Ajaccio. We had a good week or ten days at Porto, which was indeed a beautiful place, at the back of a narrow inlet between towering red rocks. The beach was white coarse sand. Walking up from the sea you came to the high point; it then sloped down again to a big fresh water lagoon with a grove of eucalyptus on the right and a cluster of houses on the left of it. The lagoon was cooler than the sea; the stream which fed it came steeply down from the mountains. There was a sort of drinking shack, which boasted a bottle of Johnny Walker Black Label, at the far end of the beach. One of the houses was the hotel-restaurant where we stayed. Jack wasn't very happy in himself. His letters from Paris had been full of doubts and worries about his life. We swam and walked and talked, and tried another nearby hotel for a meal. There to my amazement I met Maurice Charbonnel, who had resided in solitary splendour at Pachesham Towers, next to our house in Oxshott. He had been totally deaf but had moderately understandable speech and was an enthusiastic communicator. He derived his income, I believe, from the French chocolate that bears his name. He had always been happy to let me fish for roach in his lake. We all ate together and drank a lot.

I left Porto before Jack, feeling sorry to leave him, but too poor and too independent to stay. On the train from Marseille to Paris I began to feel very cold, and could not stop shivering. I went to the Bodecks and then to the nearby British Hertford Hospital. Looking back on it, I can see it was classical malaria – terrible shivering fits alternating with exorbitantly high temperatures – but it took them ten days or more to diagnose, by which time I was becoming skeletal, and could be picked up easily by a nurse and put in a bath. I actually had screens round my bed, in the manner of patients who are not long for this world, when they started giving me quinine. I began to eat – two meals at each mealtime – and after about six weeks altogether I went to stay with Ray Cortens, who had a room in the place de la Contrescarpe, very beautiful. Ray had been to see me regularly.

I had another visitor, though, while I was recovering: Campbell Kilduff, a *Herald Tribune* journalist and a very serious drinker, came to tell me that Jack Crummey was dead. He was at least as drunk as usual and kept pointing at me in my bed, saying 'You're the kiss of death! The kiss of death!' until the woman he was with took him away. Jack had died in the American Hospital, but they were not clear what of. Dengue fever was mentioned. I wonder if we had both been bitten by the mosquitoes in the eucalyptus grove and both contracted some strain of malaria which took pathologists dangerously long to identify. I thought of the lace curtains in Boston, and of how pure and nice a person Jack had been. What would his parents say? What Campbell Kilduff had said was very difficult to forget., even though it was rubbish.

The year Beryl came to see me in Corsica was my last whole academic year there, that of 1954–5. I found the Collège a little fresher looking and much more organized. The new principal was a ponderous veteran of Colditz; there were some interesting new residents besides myself; and although my timetable was more spread out over the week, I felt easier with the pupils. I often took them out into the *maquis* and taught them songs, which they preferred to the possible embarrassment of having to speak English to me. Being less anxious about money, I took two meals a day at my restaurant, and jibbed only at eating two exceedingly small birds which I was told were blackbirds from the mountains, saying that I found their song more nourishing. By this time people I met who did not know all about me – there were still a few – would say in a slightly knowing way 'It's clear that you're not from Corsica. I expect you're from the Continent.' My French had never been so good – and will never be as good again, I dare say.

The new residents were the Battistinis. He was a very jolly, friendly, tall man from Cap Corse in the northern part of the island; she from the Continent, a rather glamorous blonde. He was by way of being a surrealist poet and a friend of René Char's. He taught classics and history, was effusively hospitable, and made a film that winter involving as many of us as he could recruit: a surrealist film which I never saw, called, not *The Grapes of Wrath* but *The Water-melons of Anxiety* (*Les Pastèques de l'angoisse*). Other stars in Yves's film were Pierre Borrély, the philosophy teacher, and my friends Andrée and Suzanne, who had a flat in the wing of the Collège on the right as you faced the sea. Borrély had a room in the Hôtel César et de l'Univers which was now a lodging-house rather than an hotel. The wallpaper was monstrously impressive: a larger-than-life pattern of dark-green leaves and bananas. Borrély called it his *salon rationaliste*. It revived in his mind memories of his year's teaching in Martinique, which he had hated. The black boys had been not docile but disconcertingly confident, and had insisted on wearing hats in class. Borrély was a fine combination of simplicity and learning: on his subject he was brilliant but about life itself he was almost a child. He loved flying model aeroplanes up behind the Collège on the road to Foce, but was really frightened of the trip home by Air France. He made us all laugh a lot, but he had a big streak of melancholy and homesickness in him. He wanted to be back with his mother in Digne in the southern Alps where presumably he was looked after and told what to do all the time. Marchand and Andrée and Suzanne and I all loved him; but he almost never wrote to us after that time, whereas we four remained quite close friends.

Andrée Grandperret and Suzanne Gautherin had been together since their training college days. They both taught French, though Suzanne had studied English, about which she remained rather shy. We very quickly became friends. Lucien Marchand and Rosette were now married and had two children and lived down the steps in the town itself, but we at the Collège lived at the highest point, and overlooked Sartène from our eminence, with nothing above us but a little cemetery and the road to Foce. I grew lonely and even homesick myself at times: Andrée and Suzanne were always welcoming and sympathetic and hospitable, and still are. My children now know as well as I did all those years ago how difficult it is to pay for a drink or a meal in their company. It was Andrée and Suzanne who first introduced me to Rimbaud, whom they seemed to adore, and to Apollinaire. They would talk about 'Rimbe' as if he were a kind of phenomenal acquaintance or fellow-student from the past, and there was a big portrait of him on the wall of their living-room. They drew Lucien out of his shyness and reserve and he began to laugh aloud in cafés, both with and at them. I also came in for some teasing: they thought it very amusing that I should seriously refuse some invitation or other in the grounds that I 'had to' go to Foce. What was at Foce? It was simply a cluster of houses three or four miles up the mountain behind the Collège: a mile or two of road where, apart from a straggle of peasants coming and going on Sunday morning or Sunday evening (the men as often as not riding on small donkeys, and the women on foot carrying bundles), I remember meeting no one all the times I went up there; and then a path through *marquis* and holm oak past a spring, up to the hamlet and the look-out point where six years before a Mlle Paganelli had taught me some rudimentary Corsican dialect – a dialect of Italian rather than of French. A tough old woman in a house on a precipice near the beginning of this path had lent me a pair of binoculars on my first walk up there, saying that if I was coming back by another route I should simply leave them in Sartène for her. 'Everyone knows me,' she said.

The road to Foce is where I suppose I began to feel more than a liking for Corsica; I practically ran up it on Marchand's wedding day to get the cyclamen; and now Andrée and Suzanne tell me they are thinking of building a house on it.

47

The poet Philip O'Connor lived somewhere near the Scala Theatre in Charlotte Street with a beautiful woman called Maria. I suppose my adventures in Paris and Corsica amused him, in any case he lent me a cottage in Suffolk, the western half of Purton Hall, Purton Green, Stansfield. He even lent me his bicycle to get there. I had done a few weeks' work and had some money. I had worked in a sweet factory, about which I best remember the luxurious way we washed our hands in cocoa butter and dried them on clean cotton waste, and I liked the idea of the country, where I thought I might go on writing.

I was staying with Sadie from Central Books, who had by this time married Bruce Dunnett, with whom she was living in her father's old flat in Stamford Hill. I set off from there and rode the eighty miles to Denston, through Thaxted and Steeple Bumpstead, in a day. I had to collect the key to Purton Hall from the Denston copper-beaters, John and Joan. Luckily they put me up; I could hardly walk.

At Purton Hall I had a nice neighbour, Miss Sophie Brown, a white-haired woman whose father had been a shepherd in the same place. To illustrate her observation about sheep being difficult to look after and prone to all sorts of ailments, she nodded towards the barn next to the house and said: 'We had a great old storm one winter, and when that barn blew down you could hear the crash of medicine bottles for miles.'

We drew our water from the same well, and I cut firewood for her, while she occasionally left a baked custard on my doorstep. Inside the cottage it was dark and dusty. There was no electricity. I cooked on a paraffin stove or a Primus, or on the fire. I was too interested and busy keeping the house going to do much writing, but I remember reading an enormous leather-bound copy of *Don Quixote* with Doré illustrations, mostly by candlelight. The money soon ran out, and Miss Brown told me the farmer wanted a yard man, so I went to work for him, having first done a few days' sugar-beet topping for a farmer at Denston called Orbell.

The previous yard man was said to have left suddenly, having suffered a nervous breakdown because of the mud. There were no tractors on the farm, and I carted all the pig mash, fodder-beet and corn in a horse-drawn tumbril. To get water I had to harness a horse to the water-cart, which it disliked, and sit on the horse sideways and back it into the pond till the water-cart sank with a muffled clang. I had to hold the horse back till the cart filled up and then let it struggle out of the pond with all the weight of the water behind it, as well as the noise of the iron wheels.

I fed two lots of pigs, one yard of bullocks and the spare horses. The distances were longish, and the pig food had to be mixed and measured. Sixty buckets of water took some carrying, which I didn't mind, but the counting I did then has never quite left me. At the time it seemed to possess me: I counted not only buckets of water but steps across the kitchen when I made tea, strokes of the bread-knife when I cut bread, movements when I undressed to go to bed. Choreography, I thought, but for what ballet?

In the spring I had a malaria attack which began on top of a stack of bean straw. In hospital in Bury St Edmunds they gave me some new drug and told me to let them know if it ever recurred again.

Only two visitors appeared at Purton Hall. Peggy Rogerson came and stayed a few days; she had been a nurse at the British Hospital in Paris. She left me most of a bottle of cognac and went and started a job in the Royal Masonic Hospital. Then one evening Hugh Barrett came up the long grass track and under the oak trees and knocked on the door. He was hearty and polite and a good talker. The Grenvilles – John and Joan, the copper-beaters – had told him about me. I was pleased to have company and realized that I could learn a lot from him. He seemed to know what was going on all round the district, and he certainly understood farming. He was managing a farm called Appleacre not very far away. When he eventually left I looked at the brandy bottle, sadly depleted, and the fireplace on which he had put every single stick of firewood I had cut, and jerked my chin up with a sound of disapproval. But it had been worth it.

48

Hugh not only managed Appleacre. That year he took on pupil whom I met during harvest, while finding out about building loads on wagons and pitching sheaves, and even shocking or stooking barley. The pupil was Vic Knowland, who had read law, been to the Byam

Shaw Art School and spent nearly the whole war in India. He and his wife Lennie – they had met in the early thirties and afterwards attended the same art school – were living on the Suffolk–Essex border and looking around for a farm. I went back to Baythorn End one evening with them to help extracting honey. I was surprised and delighted to find that these kind and civilized people had large quantities of books as well as pictures, and that they were interested in what was happening in 1948 in art and literature, their appetite for that kind of thing undiminished by the passage of time or the arrival of four children since their art school days. The proms were beginning, and the Third Programme entering its great period. For the next half a dozen harvests I sweated with Vic and his men Chris and Walter Chapman all day, and listened and argued and slept under the roof of Roamwood Green Farm at night.

Lennie Knowland and her husband Vic (her first names are Irene *Lennox* Macfarlane) brought into my life something very much needed and very important. About half a generation my seniors, they stayed – being farmers – where they were, and did what they did. Not so much out of the world (since they knew what was going on, and painted and read and played music and wrote) as out of the battle, the turmoil, the exaggerated ups and downs and excitements and depressions of life in Soho and France, they helped damp down my own fluctuations between gross over- and undervaluation of myself, as the liquid in a compass bowl damps down the wilder swings of the needle. They seemed to see me more steadily than I did myself, and often in a more favourable light as well.

Hugh and Deirdre Barrett, through whom I first met the Knowlands, were similarly rock-like. They put me up at Appleacre for some weeks, and Hugh turned out to have met and much admired Anna Essinger, the Bunce Court headmistress, during the war, in connection with Quaker Relief. They both educated me about life in the country and life on the farm, and I remember Deirdre's lending me James Stephens's *Irish Fairy Tales* and a Malory *Morte d'Arthur* – both with Dulac illustrations. Their children were younger than the Knowlands' and their lives were tougher in economic terms. All of us are still friends, but I suppose that forty years ago harvest at Roamwood was a touch cushier than harvest at Appleacre. I don't mean that this applied to anyone but myself: for the women I should imagine that it was equally demanding and exhausting. It may possibly have been actually harder on Lennie, since she had more to do with the farm-work – she was partly responsible for the Jersey herd – and is perhaps a less placid person.

Vic and Lennie became a sort of point of reference for me, and I realize how true this was when I remember that I took my first wife and my second wife to see them. I was going to say and Beryl Kaye, but that is not true. I only talked about her to them, and wrote, leaning on their piano at Roamwood, a poem about the three dancers, begging Lennie to let her have the next flat to become vacant in Wilby Mews – which she did.

Of all the generosities I received from them, the greatest – apart from their constant friendship – was the little rent-free mews flat that was mine from June 1952. It was at the back of the mews, a cul-de-sac, and at the widest part of it, facing back to the road. The mews was somewhat bottle-shaped: the exit to the road was quite narrow. The flat was really small, probably too small to share with another person. It consisted of a room about twelve feet square divided diagonally into a bedroom at the back and a sitting-room at the front. The bedroom had a skylight but no view, and an exiguous bathroom gave on to it. At the top of the stairs, a long, straight flight which turned right at the top on to the first floor, the landing outside the front room was all there was for the kitchen, with a lavatory over the stairs themselves on the same level.

I moved into the mews with my first wife, Veronica. I was about to begin my final year at university. A year later we parted after two years of marriage, and I went on living in the mews until 1959, when I moved into a flat in Rosslyn Hill with Rosalind Windebank.

In the meantime I worked at the Kensal Green gasworks and for the GPO at Paddington West District Office, and had a final year in Corsica. In the autumn, winter and spring of 1957–8, Vic and Lennie lent me a big house by the water at Walberswick, and didn't mind my letting the mews flat in order to have something to live on without having to earn money. This was the best few months I think I ever had, from the point of view of writing. The year following, I was working as a copywriter in an advertising agency, where I met my second wife. Until we moved to Norfolk, we had a different flat in the same mews – again, thanks to Lennie.

49

After harvest, 1949, I stayed in various places in London and got a job working on the tramlines for the London Transport Executive, which was, like working in the gasworks in East Greenwhich, a sort of exercise in industrial archaeology. So, if it comes to that, were my jobs in Suffolk with the horses and no tractors, and at the GPO's West District Office in Paddington. But before harvest I had gone to visit Bruce in Cornwall.

At Trevithal, Paul, near Penzance, Bruce had taken a stone barn for five shillings a week and was – between jobs in a hotel, at a bakery and on various farms for a day or a week at a time – experiencing life on his own and out of London, and painting. He had moved to Cornwall at about the same time as I went to Corsica and was finding it pretty difficult. None of us had any difficulty at all finding unskilled work in London: in Cornwall small farmers tended to help each other out and not employ people. Distances were greater, and a bicycle was needed. Even then one could get very wet and cold and tired in the course of obtaining the small amount of money needed to keep going. Indulging in the luxury of creative work meant having to scrape a little money together and live meanly. And painting is more expensive than writing. I thought Bruce made almost superhuman efforts, and was glad they were productive ones.

I stayed with him for a few days in June. For two or three of them we helped Freddy Rhodda, his landlord, picking his early potatoes. We went for a drink or two to Newlyn, walked a lot, and talked a lot. One afternoon we had mackerel fetched up from Mousehole, just below Paul. The barn had a floor in it, no more than seven feet above ground level, and a ladder going up to a trapdoor, above which was the studio/living-room, with a divan and spare mattress and a good window. The space below was the kitchen and storage area.

Cornwall I remember vaguely as quaintly pretty and very rocky; and friendly – but with deep reserve. Johnny Minton used to say that he had been walking somewhere there and had asked somebody the way. 'He just looked at me and went *ffssss!*' – drawing breath hard between upper teeth and lower lip. '*Not* very maty.'

It was at about this time that Jeffrey took or invited Johnny Minton to tea with my mother, who liked him very much and said she thought it extremely generous of him to invite Jeff for a holiday in Spain. Johnny was not the only homosexual friend we made who expressed his admiration for all three of us. There was a film producer, a very nice and amusing man called Vivian Cox, who lived at Notting Hill Gate, who used to enthuse about the backs of our necks. Jeffrey says that my mother displayed extreme innocence in calling Johnny generous, but I am doubtful about this. I don't remember her expressing any warmth of feeling towards any woman or girl with whom we got involved.

I know less about her attitude towards my sister Sonia at about this time. It hadn't fundamentally changed, I'm sure, because she told me about Sonia's 'behaviour' in a very unfriendly way after I returned from Canada. While I was having malaria in Paris, my sister got married to a quiet and nice ex-RAF man in London. I was not told about it until I returned, and can't remember whether I saw them then or months later. I'm afraid she tended to bully him, and I'm afraid I found him strangely colourless; but he was extraordinarily patient with her, and unselfishly kind over my mother's illness. The wedding photograph which I somehow possess still makes me feel frightened and uneasy, perhaps because I really don't know accurately, but can only guess, what is going on between everyone in it; or in anyone's mind.

Back in London, which is to say Soho, after harvest, I stayed in various places, on people's floors, with Bobby Hunt and Marsh in a flat belonging to Susan Einzig, and at 37 Hamilton Terrace, in Johnny Minton's flat. By this time we were quite well acquainted, and he used to tease me about being so very heterosexual. I had long ago changed my mind about his being merely 'silly' and enjoyed talking with him and found him well read and sharply intelligent. Bobby and his friends Peter Dunbar (who eventually married Marsh, with whom Bobby was living when I first met them), and Oska and Rick, were all Johnny's students; Susan Einzig I saw more as a colleague. Bobby and she could draw very like Johnny, indeed Bobby did a job or two for Johnny, and is the author of one or two 'Mintons', I understand.

Johnny had a great deal of work to do, illustrations mainly. While I stayed with him I remember at least two interesting commissions: a series of designs for postage stamps, and another of illustrations for a novel by H.E. Bates, whom Johnny seemed to like and get on with.

In the evenings we went drinking locally and in Soho, or Johnny would have a party. I used to help clean up the big room overlooking the garden, where wisteria grew round the balcony and a pear tree stood to the right near the wall. Johnny would pick up a whisky bottle and speculate about the 'behaviour' it might contain. He was always inclined to be apprehensive rather than reminiscent. By contrast, the two Roberts, Colquhoun and MacBryde, spent many late mornings-after reminding each other and anyone who was about of the events of the previous night. Both attitudes had their amusement value; but Johnny enjoyed being funny at the expense of the future.

50

The tramline job was fairly hard to begin with. I started outside Sadler's Wells Theatre, where the 'pitch' was – a sort of tent made of tarpaulin stretched over a framework of wooden half-hoops – in Ted Cousins's gang. I spent all day from eight in the morning chipping tar and grout off granite setts and wood-blocks to make them usable again for 'patching' – that is, for replacing the paving round new rails and joints in the tram-track. For some reason I had taken a quite clean and respectable room in Netherhall Gardens, near Finchley Road underground, and I used to go back and have a cold bath, which when I got out of it would contain a great many small fragments of hard tar.

After a week or two I was taken on as pavior's mate to Freddy Alldred, a smallish, bright-cheeked man of perhaps fifty, with a very light clear voice, and a slight fussiness about his work, which he appeared to enjoy. He soon became both friendly and confidential, by which I mean that he would express his feelings a bit, about Ted the ganger, or the job. Once he told me to carry on with what I was doing and not look round. 'There's a man on the pavement,' says he, 'up towards Highbury direction on the other side. Keeps looking at his watch. He's *the walking bloke*.'

'Walking bloke?'

'Yesss,' whispers Fred. 'The walking foreman. From Rye Lane Depot.'

'Oh.'

It was nice being trusted, and feeling on the same side as Freddy Alldred. He seemed to me a sterling character. When we finished a big patch and I brushed it over with grout, we'd stand back and look at it. 'Now then, Oliver', he'd say, 'are you satisfied?' I'd smile and say yes, and he'd break into song:

> What is the meaning of Empire Day?
> Why do the cannons roar?
> Why does the cry 'God Save the King!'
> Echo from shore to shore?

I actually wrote to Fred from my next job in France, at St Yrieix, and received the following reply:

Feb. 15th, 1950
46, Priory Rd.
Hornsey

Dear Oliver

Just a few lines to say I have not forgotten you. Was very pleased to hear you were OK. I dare say you are settled down now have you got your own room yet it will be much nicer for you. I have been away from Ted's gang this last few week, one of the other paviors in the other gang got hurt, so I have had too take this place, it makes a change for me. We keep having fresh starters but they dont last long.

We have lost two more this week Oliver. My wifes not been up to much lately, she has had too take it very easy.

I still do the football but have not won a fortune yet. Well Oliver I dont think you do a lot of that, the boys who were working with you all wish to be remembered to you, the tram track dont alter much, they still keep going up and down. Well Oliver let me know how you are, when you have a few moments to spare, I dont stop up late of a night Oliver about Ten Oclock I retire so get my beauty sleep, I am just going now so I will say Good Night to you I

remain Yours Fred.

Once I had my own room at St Yrieix, and a stove in it, it became reasonably pleasant, and I did some work. However, it was not warm and sunny but cold and wet. 'Basile' – M. Bouvier, I should say – had moved here from Corsica, but I saw little of him. My English teacher was polite and respectable, though a sad exchange for Lucien Marchand. Still, when the spring came, I went swimming in a nearby lake called L'Etang Profond; and a French teacher called M. Robert and his wife were kind and friendly and used to have me to play tennis and talk. Claude Robert actually lent me the complete ten or twelve volumes of *À la recherche du temps perdu* and encouraged me to read it. It took me perhaps three weeks, during which I did little else.

I had had a letter from Bruce the week before Freddy's letter, saying that my mother had been in hospital with 'some sort of internal haemorrhage' but was all right now, and that Sonia had seen a specialist whom she liked – but I didn't know in what he specialized. At the end of term I got a much graver message to say that my mother had a cancer which had 'come back', and she was not expected to recover.

She was in a room off one of the wards in St Mary Abbots Hospital, Kensington, looking pale and sunken and thin. Sonia and Bruce and Jeff were there. She lifted her head and smiled weakly and said 'Here's my Corsican effort' with an attempt at gaiety.

She lasted five days and nights longer. For the last day she only breathed. Once she said she'd like a red geranium, and I ran and got a really scarlet one in the Earls Court Road. People kept coming in and making her bed. We all got tireder and tireder. At the end of her life she looked like a poor servant girl who'd been chronically overworked and undernourished; her teeth just showed between her pale lips, and two vertical lines between her eyebrows were sharply defined, as if incised. She had fought like a lioness to bring us up after my father died; she had fought to preserve her dignity; and finally she had fought, lying in this white bed, – I had hardly ever seen her lying down – to stay alive. Now it was all over.

Part Four

51

My mother has been dead now for forty-two years. I think of this period as a lifetime that is much longer than the one I have been describing. During this time I have lived with several women, been married twice and seen three of my four children born – the last out of wedlock. I was sacked for the first time in my life from my last job and then reinstated by an Industrial Tribunal. I have been in prison in the course of anti-nuclear civil disobedience activities, and have been received – only seven years ago – into the Catholic Church, 'the church of sinners', as one priest friend described it in his letter of welcome. I never thought I should reach the age my father was when he died, and I passed it eight years ago. I am a Senior Citizen and an Old Age Pensioner, and may possibly claim to be an adult. Because of all this I'm going to have to continue by swoops and gaps: there's too much material.

That the Roman Catholic Church is the church of sinners is a truth which was for a long time hidden from me. Not by friends, I hasten to add. George Barker, whose sister Monica's daughter was my first wife, was a distinguished poet and sinner himself, and very Catholic indeed. He got me to read Newman while I was at university, and gave me the *Journal of a Soul* of Pope John XXIII twenty years later. Perhaps he regarded himself as outside the Church, and that was what he meant by calling himself 'a renegade Catholic'. He was certainly delighted when, soon after visiting Assisi with him and his son Edward, I told him I was being 'instructed'. He wrote saying he wanted to be my sponsor on my reception, but was already too ill by then to make the journey.

Friends who happened to be Catholics could never, by definition, frighten me off the Church by representing it as a sort of exclusive club for the very good; but the rigours of convent education and the insistence on Sin with a capital S (and a worse than capital punishment in store) have frightened or depressed or repelled many people I have known. I was bound to pick up a lot of anti-Catholic feeling in all my schools except the Jewish one; in most of the newspapers; among the political lefties of my youth; even in the Christian Science Church, as far as I heeded it at all. (I was in the same Sunday School class as Glynis Johns.) This meant that to enter a Catholic church except in France or Italy was a slightly terrifying thing to do: my brother Bruce told me a month or two ago that the Requiem Mass for George Barker's memorial service at the London Oratory was the first Catholic Mass he had ever attended. In England in the fifties at least, RC churches seemed, if you just happened to slip inside one at random, to be strong on the odour of sanctity – sometimes literally so – and weak on taste in, for example, statuary. Worst of all, the English Catholics, so long persecuted and reviled, seemed to have developed a defensive rectitude, severity even, which was as remote from the smile of Pope John as the word Sin with a capital S is from the word love with a lower-case l. It will be clear from this that I could never have reached the Church unless I had got a sort of unspoken message of welcome from it, and felt that there might be more to celebrate in it than to feel bad about.

Some clubs exclude you by disqualification; others by their membership subscriptions. Generally speaking, Soho was for me a very large and heterogeneous club. I won't say church, though the parallel is there somewhere. The entrance fee to Tony's in Charlotte Street was the price of a cup of tea; the same as to the Alexandria Café in Rathbone Place. To the pubs, it was the price of a half of bitter, or even mild, if you could keep your mind off the ullage. It became clear though that there were advantages in clubs. You could avoid football supporters and tourists, for instance. The Caves, the Colony, the Gargoyle and the Mandrake all charged some sort of subscription. To the Colony, which was run by the unforgettable and unrepeatable Muriel Belcher, I preferred for a long time to be 'signed in' by a member who was there when I asked for him or her, or who took me there. My brother Bruce was on the committee in the sixties, and before that John Minton, Lucian Freud and Francis Bacon – its most suitable and indeed cherished member – all obliged at one time or another, as did Elizabeth Smart. I visited the Gargoyle more rarely. With its Matisse mirrors and its rather secretive lift, it was the most elevated of all Soho clubs, and its prices, though not high, were the highest of the four. I never subscribed to or became a member of the Gargoyle, though I liked it very much.

To the Mandrake, downstairs in Meard Street, and so vast and sprawling that you expected it to connect soon with Piccadilly Circus underground, I did, I think, pay a subscription once or even twice. It was run by Boris Watson, who was said to have been in prison for the manslaughter of a customer of the old Coffee An' near St Giles's Church, with a sabre. He was large and usually placid, a bit bossy, and capable of being cross in a dinner-ladyish way, but I never saw him angry. In the Mandrake I met the poets Allen Ginsberg and Gregory Corso – I rather think they were with George Barker – and Dylan Thomas. Corso was not too amusing at the time; he would go on about how 'high' he'd been last night, and last week, and last year. Dylan was in very good form and being naughty, witty, charming and comical – really irresistible, and much more confident than when I first met him in the Duke of York with Caitlin, when he bought me a drink or two and inquired rather seriously whether I wrote verse. Caitlin said something ill-tempered to me, probably supposing me to be one of those people – perhaps I was – who was depriving her of Dylan or/of his/her money. I don't know. Anyway I was bold enough to be as rude back, so she slapped my face, quite convincingly. I had the last word, and a nasty one it was; I don't like to remember it. I'm afraid this cut short the conversation.

It was the Caves that became my walk-in club. I paid one or two subscriptions and then forgot. The club was on ground-floor level and had a sort of chucker-out whose job was really only to sit and ask people coming in whether they were members. Secondo Carnera, enormous but very gentle, had only to walk round the bar and on to the floor to send anyone into retreat. At first, in my memory, it was run by a man called Frank. It was taken over from him by Jenny, a rather made-up, vivacious and vulnerable person who could be both sympathetic and sympathy-seeking.

Into the Caves came pretty nearly the whole of 'Soho': the two Roberts (Colquhoun and MacBryde), Paul Potts, David Archer, the poet Sidney (W.S.) Graham, with Nessie Dunsmuir his wife and his brother Alistair, Peter Brook alias Anthony Carson, Nina Hamnett, Nelson Pollard, Rosalind Windebank, Terry Gilby, her friend Pat, Michael Winters, Bob Katz, Janet Rumble, Frank Norman, Michael Piper and Lily Heidsieck, Michael Summerskill, Tony Kingsmill, Tony Cronin, John Raymond and even Paul Johnson. Like the Colony (almost next door) and the Mandrake, it opened at three o'clock (the closing-time for pubs after lunch), but I think it closed earlier than either the Mandrake or the Colony. Because it was large and dimly lit, there was space and sometimes quiet. In it, it was possible to move from one end to the other and talk with an entirely different collection of people. To do that in the smaller Colony Room, you had to stay much closer to people, and be more intimate. The Caves customers were a much more loosely knit family.

The most – perhaps the only – unpleasant memory I have of the Caves is of an early summer evening in 1958, at the time when Stephen Spender caused *Encounter* to publish a long Apollinaire translation of mine, *The Song of the Ill-Loved*. The fee was impressive, since they paid by the line: it is a matter of nearly 300 lines. Paul Potts was standing at one end of the bar, and as I bought a drink for Rosalind and myself, he suddenly screamed: 'Here's Stephen Spender's little sexy boy!'

I could hardly believe it. I paid for the drinks and decided to go downstairs to the gents. While I was gone, Rosalind remonstrated with him. 'Sir!' I presume she said. 'Mister Potts! That is no way to speak to someone who has done you no harm!' Whereupon Potts kicked her hard in the shins and departed.

I don't know what went on behind his saintly and dome-like forehead. I'd always thought him rather intense and sometimes pompous. But this nastiness was really indigestible. I heard afterwards that there was worse. John Stephens, an actor-poet who worried about his dark good looks, came into the York Minster one evening practically weeping: he had put Potts up for a few days. Potts had robbed him of – I'm not sure – shirts and books, I suppose; and when reproached had abused him. Just now, in the street, Paul had shouted at him, calling him a 'damned half-caste'. It was really too much. I avoided speaking to Paul Potts for the rest of his life. When I saw Christopher Barker's photograph of him in *Portraits of Poets* I felt what an awful life he must have had, and I was sorry. I went to his funeral more punctiliously than I should have gone to that of a friend. But for me Paul Potts's mind is a mystery I am in no special hurry to solve.

More comically, I was, in 1954 or thereabouts, very much taken with Terry Gilby, and used to talk to her in the Caves. She somewhat mischievously talked back with a most serious air, though I found it impossible to persuade her to come with me to some other place to continue our conversation more quietly. Janet, another friend of Terry's and Rosalind's, told me that it would be difficult to get anywhere with Terry, since Rosalind would never permit it. The implication was that Rosalind was a sort of bossy lesbian. In fact, it was Terry herself who was a lesbian. Darkly and threateningly, according to Rosalind, I confronted her – asking her even (I have got over my embarassment by now – Rosalind has recounted it to so many of our mutual friends) *if she would like to 'come outside'*. This afforded much amusement to the whole gang of Rosalind's friends at the time. It was also one of those moments of intense antagonism that sometimes precede closer acquaintanceships and even affection. Terry Gilby gave us both a great deal of pleasure when in 1957 she came and spent a few days with us in the house in Walberswick, in her donkey jacket and black cords, with her big greenish eyes under her dark fringe, rolling her own cigarettes and drinking quiet pints in the Anchor. One day she agreed to put on a violet-coloured dress of Rosalind's, and came downstairs looking really enchanting. By that time I liked Terry for *who* she was, and realized that *what* she might be was no business of mine.

52

I didn't meet Veronica, at that time known to everyone as Wendy, in Soho, but at a party during my first year at Goldsmiths' given by Glyn Collins and Walter McElroy, two American friends of George Barker's, somewhere near South Kensington, I think. I was at the end of a most drawn-out and painful 'being in love'. During my mother's last illness, Bruce had written to say that Kay Bush – for whom I had waited so long in Coventry Street Corner House – had been very kind and helpful. Unfortunately it wasn't Kay but a showgirl my mother had met and been friendly with in the theatre, called Marie Foster. I don't know if her coming to the hospital several times and being sympathetic and friendly with us was what gave my pursuit of her this intensity, but whatever it was, Marie was probably unaware of it. I suppose she was a little bit interested in me, and found it difficult to say that I was not right for her, or whatever she might have said. Anyway I dangled after her quite absurdly for a long time, spending money I couldn't afford on buying her a ring, and treasuring a medallion of St Jude she had given me. Finally, in the new year of 1951, I found she had another man, and left her very angrily and abruptly. I was glad to be free.

It was time I met Wendy, who was young and shy-mannered but candid, when she did venture to speak. I paid a lot of attention to her, though it wasn't always easy to talk with her because she seemed unresponsive and passive, being shy. She was certainly a shining person then, and I remember being very put out when David Wright began to take a close interest in her. I had known and liked him for a long time, but his being a recognized and recognizable poet, and a most charming fellow on top of that, increased my jealousy and irritation.

At college, which I attended pretty regularly and seriously (there were no days free of lectures on my general degree course), I was taken a fancy to by a student who was in many ways the opposite of Wendy, physically and in character. She got me to meet her because she said she wanted to ask me something, then she kept putting me off. On our third meeting she came back to my sister's flat where I had a room, for tea. What she wanted to ask me, it turned out, was whether I would kiss her. So things became complicated in a way that was sadly familiar. My daily sixty-five lengths of the New Cross Baths swimming-pool, and my reading in Latin and English and French and history, which the swimming was intended to make it possible for me to get on with without having to think about exercise for the rest of the day – even my fairly regular pub and party going in the evenings – were not sufficient to take the edge off my appetite for sex. I went to bed with both her and Wendy for seven or eight weeks, not feeling too badly about it, since I concealed it from neither of them, but disturbed in my own mind by this excessiveness, and without any sort of honourable intentions, or even dishonourable ones. I was anxious about my course work, anxious about money, anxious about Jeffrey's being on the run from the army, and anxious about my sister and her husband, in whose flat I was staying, paying precious little rent and doing a certain amount of housework to make up for it.

In Soho life went on at a rapid pace. So it did at 23 Stanhope Gardens, George Barker's parents' house near Gloucester Road, where Wendy was living. In February the husband of his sister Eileen died. She was John Fairfax's and Barry's mother.

Sunday February 4. Finished reading *Manon Lescaut* before lunch to which Bruce and Jeff came. Tea first with Sonia & then with Mamma [George's mother]. Then Guinness & port = black velvet and long talk with 'Bonpa' [George's father]. Finally HH Finch at Notting Hill Gate w. Wendy. Roberts & Sidney there, then Jeff & Pete [Arthy]. Then to Roberts' with Wendy. Sang. Finally taxi to Stanhope Gdns. Walked home. Wendy is just fine. Roberts are only homosexual, not inhospitable. Wendy must vigorously dry her hair and go to bed. Driving rain this morning and tonight. But eventually home at last. Read first part of novel called *As It Was*.

Monday February 5. Finished *As It Was . . . World Without End* this morning. Trevor Fisher sent £2. I went via Ktsbridge (Powells statuary yd.) to town, Malta, Mandrake, Madrid. 4.30 pm Mamma's. Lot of strained atmosphere and Eileen & children. Walter [McElroy] told me her husband died last night. Wendy came, George came, David W[right] came. Set about trying to talk. Children eventually went to bed. All to Denmark. David Archer came and went. Wendy hesitated on stairs a long time. George came out and went round to Americans; John [Fairfax], Barry, Eileen, George, David W., me; & drank rum and water & sang, mostly badly. 'When Irish Eyes' made her cry at last. She left with Barry. George went on singing. John was going to bed, Walter and Glyn got all officious. I left and got back at 2, cleaned and assembled candlestick, went and made a Welsh rarebit. Now bed at last.

Tuesday February 6. Latin. Horace with Handford. Mamma's, town to see Bruce, too late. Phoned Nevern Mansions: no answer, so [W. & I] came. They were just back. S. cooked a meal we didn't want. Felt tired, angry, frustrated, importuned, tired. Took W. home. Washed up & went to bed early. But did not go to sleep at once.

Wednesday February 7. 6 p.m.: As I was doing the kitchen 2 (plain clothes) police arrived for Jeff. I could give them no satisfaction. Saw Jeff in Soho drunk with Peter. He looks like a naughty little boy who is ashamed. The army is hell but this delinquency is no good. MIDNIGHT: Everything is, as I hope, all right. At Keydrich's [Rhys] suggestion and with Jeff's approval or acquiescence at least (& to his relief) I sent a telegram to Catterick saying he was ill, certificates following. So I hope things are all right or will be. He had a lot of money. When Wendy & I got home W. gave me £1 – from Jeff. He'd asked her not to give it me till then. I was surprised and touched indeed. Talked to John [Fairfax] who thank God seems all right now. Read half of the *Iliad* (Rieu) today. Wendy vomited halfway up the stairs in the Black Horse. I mopped it up. She was better afterwards.

Thursday February 8. W. came round and I had my tie off before she explained. She was very silent and guilty looking. I read the *Iliad* to her and we had supper. I said I didn't like waiting on her and told her to wash up. We parted smiling & yet sadly. I went up town to see Jeff. He's not been to the doctor but has some idea of going to Cornwall. The only way to finish it is surely within the law. Sidney Graham arrived drunk at Tony's. I left my overcoat there, forgetting it. It rained all night. S. & I went to knock up company & drink but couldn't. Stood in David Wright's doorway talking, singing. It rained in the hospital courtyard. I waited in the Corner House for the 3.33 a.m. bus, with Ted Belgrave & Harry D [Diamond]. Home at 4 a.m. wet through.

In April Wendy missed her period and in June we were married. I stopped seeing Kay, the college student. Wendy and I had nowhere to live at first, and spent a lot of time looking for flats. In the vacation, after the intermediate exams, we went to Vic and Lennie's. In August Wendy had a miscarriage. Her suffering was intense and prolonged. I had probably been wrong to marry her for the reason I did (the local doctor said she could not have been as much as four months pregnant), and now I was unable to contemplate leaving her. We went to live for three months in an old Thames barge belonging to Vic and Lennie at Blackshore, Southwold. We had Donald and Renée Horwood for neighbours, and the Harbour Inn for our local pub. The barge was beautiful, if a bit damp, and walking across the marshes to Southwold was always extraordinary though often cold and wet. Sam Adamson the council man had to deal with an invasion of rats, and from then on was a reliable visitor. Jeffrey and his first wife Anna (who had attempted suicide on 3 October) came and spent Christmas with us in the barge. At the new year (1952) we got a room in Arundel Gardens, W11. Commuting at the weekends was a strain on both of us. I hitch-hiked every time, usually from Gallows Corner, Romford, up the A 12. I took to going back on Monday morning, since I was becoming more and more dissatisfied with the French lectures, and could generally get to Goldsmiths' by lunchtime.

Arundel Gardens was pleasant: we had a big room with a partitioned-off kitchen and a great many visitors. With a bit of difficulty, Wendy got another bookshop job. I began to work at a café in the Portobello Road on Saturdays. The merry-go-round of Soho and the Gloucester Road and South Kensington and Notting Hill Gate pubs continued. I still saw a great deal of the two Roberts. I'd gone to Tilbury with MacBryde just before our wedding to Johnsons' Wax a seventy-foot mural of his on the P & O liner *Oronsay*. I kept an eye on the private galleries as well as visiting the Tate and the National Gallery. And college was busy and interesting, if sometimes annoying. I began to write verse, and in February wrote a short poem in the Monday morning French lecture. In April Wendy and I went to see George Barker and Betty Cass at Hearne Cottage, Anstedbrook, Haslemere – near Tennyson's house at Blackdown. Wendy and I were getting on fairly badly: when I look at my diary I find it absolutely full of activity and of anxiety, particularly about money. Waiting for grant cheques, borrowing money in small amounts, and lending it too – all these things caused huge and disproportionate anxieties which I passed on to Wendy. I notice we had a happy day or so now and then, when I received money and we could pay the rent and our small debts; then we returned to gloom, frustration and dissatisfaction. Even George's encouraging me about poetry did not help. I was in a sort of swamp of guilt and angst; Wendy mainly reminded me, without ever mentioning it, of my wrongness and stupidity.

We moved into the little mews flat in June 1952, but nothing helped. Money wasn't really the problem. Thinking about it now, I realize it would have been the same if we'd had twice as much. We'd have gone on having people to meals, and going out, and drinking and having what's called a good time, but the whole business would have simply accelerated. We eventually escaped from each other a year later. Wendy went off to Corsica with a friend of George's after I had begun to stay out, here and there, with people in Soho. When my final exams came along, I was busy writing a long and mostly regrettable poem about what I felt for Wendy. I couldn't quite believe I'd got even the Third Division pass I did obtain.

53

Walter Chapman, who with his brother Chris used to work at Vic Knowland's first farm (and before that for 'old Boone' who had said during the war that he liked the Americans, but why did they want to bring them whoite men with 'em?), was the strongest man I ever worked with, I suppose. Butch, the foreman on the *Daily Worker* site, walked up a long ladder with no hands, carrying a bag of cement on his back, but Walter was no show-off. If he threw a stone, it made a loud humming sound and went out of sight. He handled nineteen-stone sacks of wheat with a smooth familiarity. He was a most straight-faced joker as well. He'd walk into the Trowel and Hammer in Wetherup Street every weekday evening and look round the room – the old man would go and get your drink in the beer store, there was no bar – and say 'Warm agin!' You had to be there several times, in various weathers and seasons, to appreciate the value of the remark, which was his invariable evening greeting. Twenty years after he left the farm-work, which was ill enough paid even though Vic paid above 'the rate', to work for ICI in Stowmarket, when the Trowel and Hammer had already been closed for a few years, I went into the nearest pub and asked (it was lunch-time) whether Walter came in there.

'Yes. Walter Chapman comes in here.'

'Does he still say "Warm agin"?'

'Yes,' said the landlord, brightening. 'Thass his word.'

What made me think of Walter was the idea that when I first went to Soho for tomato purée and fresh spaghetti, Soho for me was all within a stone's throw of the intersection of Frith Street and Old Compton Street. In other words it stretched from Berwick Street to Charing Cross Road and from Gerrard Street to Soho Square, a gridiron with strong North-South bars and rather weaker East-West ones. After the acquaintance became closer, I mentally joined Soho and Fitzrovia, on the two sides of Oxford Street. Crossing Oxford Street was like having to break cover: once headed north up Rathbone Place, or south down Soho Street, I felt safe again.

But of course Soho isn't geography but anthropology, as John Heath-Stubbs most properly suggests by inventing the name *Fitzravia*, and making it rhyme with as well as comment on *behaviour*. If I were fit to do so, I should commemorate, besides the poets and painters, not the smart, or the well-known, or the moneyed, but those habitués without whom Soho would never have existed – for me, at any rate. People who, in Ray Cortens's words, were 'interesting or beautiful' and people who were neither spectacularly, but whom I now miss: deaf Ronny, who talked by means of slips of paper; Mac the Busker, with his generosity and his rasping voice; Jimmy Telfer, with his poor-Scots humour and slight desperation; Lily Heidsieck and Michael Piper, a wonderful pair of anguished lovers whom Peter Brook once called 'bed and breakfast'; Cyril Arapov the cameraman and distinguished photographer, as civilized as Isaiah Berlin, and modest and charming with it; Jack Green the garrulous, whom the Roberts brothers used to call Giacomo Verdi; tough Laraine the piss-artist and Eric Gillingham the anarchist, both haunters of the Rutting Shed, the last pub in Old Compton Street before Charing Cross Road; and bitterly funny Alan Stokes, who saw sometimes distorted, sometimes cruelly clearly, through his spectacles with the one cracked lens. If I could celebrate four people, they would be Gilbert Wood, Jimmy the Baker, Stephen Fothergill and Bill Belton. All of them but Jimmy came to Veronica's and my wedding reception; all of them but Stephen are not to be found any more.

Gilbert Wood painted scenery at one of those film studios north-west of London. I first met him in the late forties. He drank a lot and smoked a lot, so that his laughter was a frighteningly wheezing, choking affair, and I once, having told him something funny on an underground train going home, really believed he would do what I wished for him – eventually – which was to die laughing. He had long white hair, which fell about his face when he was drunk, rather in the manner of Elizabeth Smart's hair, come to think of it. He had the greatest respect for my brother Bruce, who must have been fifteen or twenty years his junior. 'Integrity!' he wheezed, walking less than straight along the last bit of pavement to his house one night, 'Integrity! That's what Bruce has got!' And he made tea, with a drop of whisky. He was very good at the wedding reception, and afterwards rather concerned for Wendy. He talked a lot about some fantasy of his to do with 'solid trombone playing', which seemed tremendously funny at the time, and he stared straight at Wendy, pointing with his free finger, and said: 'Don't forget. When the old man swipes, duck!'

Jimmy the Baker played draughts in Tony's in Charlotte Street, and later in the Alexandria Café. He had a rather rubbery face. He could be dour and gloomy and harsh, and he could also be hugely and sunnily smiling. He was something of a philosopher, less detached than Quentin Crisp and not camp at all, but just as wise in his way, which was a Belfast craftsman's way: his fingers and thumbs were markedly spatulate, whether or not from kneading dough, and his comments about the world were severe and disenchanted. He would always lend and borrow small sums of money with gravity, and it was a pleasure – a kind of pleasure – to repay him. He hardly ever got drunk, but was said to be capable of very violent behaviour when he did. One of the last times I saw him, he had had his teeth out, and had, besides, injured his hand. 'Ah well, now I've got nothing to fight with and nothing to bite with!' he said, and limped off down Old Compton Street, still, I felt, formidable, cheerful, small and close-cropped as ever.

Stephen Fothergill is still alive, and I feel I ought to ask his permission to say anything at all about him. Even the phrase still alive – the Emperor Caligula's last words – ought perhaps to be scrutinized. But I shall have to risk it. I certainly met him in the late forties, and saw a great deal of him before and after I first went to Corsica. He lived for a long time in Delamere Terrace, between Paddington and Maida Vale, over Lord Hills Bridge, and gave amusing parties with lots of jazz and dancing. He knew all the musicians and was for years learning to play the trumpet. His manner of speaking and his appearance would not have led you to suppose that these things were very close to his heart: he was and is a very elegant speaker of English and a most soberly attired person. But he has a great deal of charm; he is extraordinarily polite in conversation; he is friendly and amusing and disarmingly sincere. If ever I need to remind myself of the virtues of constancy and good manners, or of the fact that people can hold very different views from my own without its actually mattering (this threatens to be a silly sentence), I *always* need to remember these things – what I mean is, I'm always glad to see Stephen, because he reminds me of them.

Bill Belton's real name was Henry Belton, but no one ever used it. He lived in the same block of flats in Notting Hill Gate as Wyndham Lewis, and for a long time in the late forties and early fifties he and his charming and fittingly named wife Blossom used to entertain on Sunday nights. Besides painting and drinking, Bill was an accomplished pianist: his evenings usually included quite satisfying chunks of improvisation, often on Brahms themes. Wicked MacBryde seriously informed Wendy one night that Bill didn't actually play the piano. When she looked surprised, as he intended, he said confidentially: 'No-o . . . that's a *pianola* . . . you see?'

I got into the habit of walking to the tube with Bill when the pubs – we were usually in the York Minster – closed in the evening. We sometimes stopped for coffee on the way. He had an outrageous manner as of a naughty public schoolboy, and talked aggressively and absurdly about flogging, bare bottoms and so on. He liked calling people 'Sah!' and would on occasion address a woman as 'Madam, sah!' Behind that theatrical machinery he was thoughtful, and worried a lot about what was happening to the country, firm only in his distrust of what was not yet called 'the Establishment'.

I suppose what I like or love about all these people is, in their entirely different styles, their dependability. They do not seem to me so very different from the saints themselves, because they remain real to me and are people I can completely trust.

54

I met my second wife Jackie while I was working at Notley Advertising, Hill Street, Mayfair. Being an advertising copywriter was for a long time an option I did not have the courage to take up, despite my chronic poverty. Once I had friends like Michael White, who took over from Wendy and me the room in Arundel Gardens when we moved into the mews, and Ralph and Julian Abercrombie, and Elizabeth Smart, it was perfectly possible for me to set about getting a job; but until I acquired a little confidence as a writer I did not want to roll my career down that particular slope, however smooth. John Heath-Stubbs's tutorials in the Black Horse, George Barker's mordant and stimulating criticism, Walter de la Mare's encouragement, and even Joyce Grenfell's acceptance of advice all helped me to become more self-reliant. At the Old Yacht Yard, Walberswick, I was able to write a great deal, for me, after spending my first few months there doing absolutely nothing but keep an eye on the state of the tides and the weather and read every book in the place. The year before, I had worked as a postman at the big district office next to Paddington Station, and been published for the first time in *Encounter*. After a nice lunch with Stephen Spender and Dom Moraes, I had taken Dom into Soho for the first time, and spent a good deal of time walking about Bayswater with him, talking and listening. He had asked me what I thought of Apollinaire, and lent me a copy of *Alcools*. From Walberswick I sent poems to magazines, and my first collection around publishers; I wrote long lecture-letters to Joyce Grenfell, and visited Oxford to read poems, and to meet Peter Levi, who treated me with great generosity and kindness. The first person I remember actually calling me a poet was a retired RAMC lieutenant-colonel from the Indian Army, an amateur bookbinder who lived in Walberswick near the Anchor, and whom I met there regularly for a before-dinner drink, Colonel Newcomb. 'What are you having, poet?' he'd ask. He bound a first edition of George Barker's *True Confession* for me, and a Catullus (in violet-coloured leather), which I gave to Rosalind Windebank. She and her friends visited me at the Yacht Yard, and when I returned to London in the autumn of 1957 I became part of a sort of triangular friendship involving her and a young scientist whom I liked and still like very much. It was I suppose a very stimulating and exciting and painful experience for Lewis and myself to be involved with Rosalind, and I remember writing poems about both of them, but it didn't so much drive me into advertising as make it even more complicated and difficult for me to pursue any clear course of action.

At that time Rosalind had a Freudian analyst whom she visited on Mondays. This was in fact her chief occupation, and the whole week was geared to it. Her close friends were all aware of this and found themselves discussing psychological matters in pubs and clubs with a certain facility. Indeed Rosalind exerted a strong influence on her circle and could make most of us consider each other – and ourselves – as more or less interesting cases. Obviously there was a great deal of amusement to be had from this: Janet Graham and Terry Gilby were very skilful at extracting it. Of course to be 'analytic' in an amateur Freudian sense about writing and painting can become silly and irritating if too closely pursued. Art is synthetic and not analytic, and if sanity means giving up art, an artist must have the common sense to choose madness. The tension produced by such contradictions I found quite enjoyable. Other people simply saw danger and shied off, even going so far as to embrace the notion that one should let one's mind alone and pull oneself together. Psychology is a waste of time! But time does, just, waste, whether you believe in psychology or not.

Ralph Abercrombie, who had tried to save David Archer's Greek Street bookshop from, well, David Archer, gave me excellent advice about applying for advertising jobs. The letter I wrote obtained me three or four interviews at different agencies. When I chose Notley's, and told Julian Abercrombie that Marchant Smith was the copy director, she looked – for the only time I ever saw it – frightened. All I had seen was a quite affable, suave and highly intelligent person of small stature, rather smoothly dressed in grey, and with the slightly poached eye of the man about town – Edwardian, I thought him. But Julian told me the story of Marchant and the female account executive.

One afternoon in another agency, Marchant was proceeding down a long corridor when a woman account executive appeared at some distance, walking towards him. ('Marchant *hates* women in business,' said Julian.) When she was about ten feet from him, she slipped on the highly polished floor and landed in an undignified heap. Marchant did not stop, or even alter the pace of his progress, but as he passed her he looked down and sideways without turning his head and said: 'A curtsy would have sufficed.'

Here is a letter to Joyce Grenfell in which I observe traces of simplicity as well as of censorship for her sake, but they are slight enough to ignore. The writer is thirty-two.

C/o Cecil D. Notley Advertising Ltd. 16 IV 58
15/17 Hill St., W.1. (TEL: GROsvenor 9070 Extn 208)

Dear Joyce,

Here I have come to work early; no one else is in the office, everything is clean. It is twenty-five past nine, Wednesday morning, the sixteenth of April. Forecast: rather cold. Indeed I shall be grateful for the end of winter. The Plane trees in Berkeley Square are as bare as February, my friends in Highbury have no daffodils this year: – well, a dozen instead of a host. My oil stove hasn't been out for weeks, except by accident.

And here is my first colleague: Guy Sneath, a middle-aged copywriter going thin in front, writes histories of firms and tells stories of his previous agencies. Quiet, dullish, pleasant enough. He is beginning work by reading an old *Lilliput*. How I used to like that magazine, eighteen years ago. Sneath reads my *Manchester Guardian* after lunch, he never seems to get a paper himself.

My other two are an Oxford poet called Lucie-Smith and a new man. Lucie-Smith is chatty and collects antiques and lives with his mother; his poems are quite nice, a bit old-fashioned, a bit literary; veils of literature swathe the subject. Except in one or perhaps two poems which I not only like but quite admire. Lucie-Smith spends most of his time writing about furniture.

Well, this is an advertising agency. I've been here a month and I like it. My copy director is a somewhat Mr. Norris-ish character called Marchant Smith; he wrote some very famous Jaeger advertisements about thirty years ago, in a sort of twenties slang. He is witty and 'bored' and a bit decadent. Urbane: he brings in tit-bits from the papers and reads them in a drawl under raised eyebrows: 'Don't you find that charming?' he says. Every morning we knock at his door (his office has a carpet and a large case full of travel books) to say good morning. This is a way of saying we have arrived – on time. At least I've never been late except when my tube-train got stuck in a tunnel. Lucie-Smith is often a few minutes late and tends to sulk just a bit when told off. Apart from insisting on 9.30 a.m. Marchant leaves us alone pretty much (though one can reckon on about one visit a day with the *Times* or whatever it is). This of course leaves out his real job and my real job: he gives me advertisements to write and looks them over when done, making amendments when he feels like it or when it is necessary. But I've only done about five days' work in this month: writing invitations for Wolsey-Lombardi's dress show, and ads for rust-preventing paint, and ads for insect-repellent lamps, and inventing a name for prepacked chickens, and doing some roughs for television films (Clark's children's shoes).

I started here at the 'nominal' (trainee) salary of £500 but if things go well (they appear to be going very well, Marchant Smith says 'You appear to be going Great Guns Mr. Bernard. I think these are very good; we're very glad to have you here.') – I think I shall take a plunge and ask for More; that £500 gets to me as £8 per week, Après le taxe perçu.

I have a friend here called Sarzy, too; her name is Miss Sarzano and she writes Nylon ads, very nice ones; she is vague and somewhat laughable and erratic, has been here too long to take any notice of Marchant's love of punctuality, she gulps when she talks and falls over things rather. I think she is rather interestingly bad-looking, and as sharp as a needle with all that uncoördination.

Well, Joyce, this is the first job I've ever had which I quite liked doing, and which demands a certain ability on my part other than muscular and attentive, and which promises some sort of financial rewards. I wonder how unconvincing or unconvinced I sounded even as lately as three years ago when I said I wanted to get a decent job; and how much of my distrust of advertising was really a distrust of my own abilities as a writer. Well, I *can* write advertising copy. Now I just want to get quite good at it and be quite well-paid for it, perhaps get an office to myself somewhere at the top of the building and be out of the way but always accessible to social calls, and write a poem when I can.

Not impossible: I've done it already; at any rate I've added 30 lines to a 190-line poem (called HIS CHANSON FOR ROLAND) and done other things: oh yes – typed out 60 pages of poems for the Eyre and Spottiswoode book NEW POEMS 1959, I don't know if they are going to take them. Rupert Hart-Davis was again very nice but Negative. Edwin Muir is going to edit this E & S book: I don't know.

Anyway all these things I did here at Notley's, which everyone I know in advertising said would be the nicest possible agency for me to work at, so wasn't it lucky they offered me a job on the spot when I went to see them. And it *is* a nice place.

I think I am moving to Hampstead this year to share a flat with my friend Rosalind Windebank, if this is possible. I am losing Wilby Mews anyway, pretty soon. Rosalind is 26 and has never left home; has been ill, in mental hospital, going to analysis, etc. Is better, and deo gratia will go on getting better and be able to take a job in 6 months' time. She has a very hard fight for sanity, and finds it almost impossible to meet people etc (travel on buses etc), even at this late date. Anyway if I can manage to be a friend to her and not lose courage or patience, it might be a successful thing for her.

I am hire-purchasing a new suit, I haven't seen it yet; I suppose I shall look very suave or soigné to you, compared with my former state. Well, I don't mind looking decent all day.

News of you??? The *Guardian* doesn't follow you round the USA as they do round these parts. I can't even remember your exact date of return, but it won't be a minute too soon and you are WELCOME from me. Love to you Joyce

– Oliver

By June or July, after four months at Notley's, I had arrived late more than a dozen times. 'I'm sorry I'm late, Marchant.' 'Well, you shouldn't be late,' he'd snap. About the fifteenth time (there were tensions; there was drinking) I was still a little intoxicated from the night before and didn't care. I came in at about 10.15 and went and sat at my typewriter, pulling out a piece of yellow paper, as in Stevie Smith's title, and, I don't know, perhaps starting another letter. Marchant came in with *The Times* folded in four and I looked up and said: 'Hello Marchant, isn't it a marvellous day? I actually walked most of the way. "Earth has not anything to show. . . ."'

'Delightful,' said Marchant.

There was a typist in the corner of the room. 'Miss Jones,' he said, 'kindly take a letter: "Dear God! the very houses seem asleep. . . ."'

The whole office, and Marchant himself, so much enjoyed this, that he went out again with the paper still unquoted from.

Sarzy was, like Rosalind, 'in analysis', but she was in addition a keen and proselytizing amateur of astrology. For her Rosalind was 'A Tawny Lioness,' and I an Archer, a marksman who sometimes used poison-tipped arrows, and fired remarks at the management 'from' as she said 'your secure position in the gutter'. She could get very cross at times, though her warmth was extraordinary, and her generosity almost disastrous. I remember her forcing me – and indeed Rosalind, who joined the firm for six months, after the experiment with the flat in Hampstead had failed – to take large spoonfuls of disgusting powdered gelatin in glasses of rather nice Vouvray. 'You need protein!' she hissed. 'Both of you!'

It was Sarzy who first told me about Jackie, who was 'an enchanting person, a dancer. She sometimes does a bit of modelling for Clarks [shoes]. Oh Oliver, you'd adore her!' And so it was, in the summer of 1959: we met at a party given by Bridget Gibbings, Robert Gibbings's daughter, where I also met the man Jackie was then living with. I failed to warm to him. It would have been difficult even for Sarzy to exaggerate Jackie's attractiveness and niceness and fineness. Apparently she performed the same or a similar piece of *private relations* work about me to Jackie. And she and Stanley Brooks, a young and spry Notley director with a sense of humour, came and witnessed our marriage at Chelsea Register Office, taking us to lunch in a taxi at an Italian restaurant in Kensington Church Street, on 12 October 1959.

By the time I met Jackie I myself was 'in analysis', or at least a version of it, attending the Tavistock Clinic, an institution for which I have nothing but praise, and which I believe to have been maintained or at least substantially supported by Marks & Spencer's money. My group analyst was Dr Malan, who removed the mistrust inspired by his unfortunate name (at that time associated with South African apartheid) in a few minutes, and whom I owe thanks I could hardly at the time have meaningfully conveyed, since all patients tend to regard their Freudian analysts as *in loco parentis boni*, and not merely *in loco parentis*. I arrived for the first session in an exacerbated version of my growing anxiety. My sister Sally – Sonia – was by this time undergoing the fate of involuntary patients diagnosed as schizophrenic: drugs, ECT and brass locks; long and miserable green-painted corridors; doctors whose affected infallibility grew in proportion to their ignorance of the individual case. It seemed at that time – and I don't know how much or how little things have altered in thirty-odd years – that there was no such thing as a truly individual case because it was thought that that sort of thing was probably limited to people with money, or perhaps to isolated and spectacular freak cases which might be useful for teaching purposes.

I went once a week, and Marchant didn't like it much; but by then I was going even 'Greater Guns' as a copywriter. I had begun working on a whole group of rather despised accounts at Notley's, and was shortly to win a copywriting prize for the agency's credit and my own financial advancement for a self-tapping screw advertisement. My engineering accounts, so much looked down upon by the other copywriters engaged in selling products that I thought had none of the glamour with which they were credited (consumer products whose makers invested hugely in advertising), appealed strongly to me, mainly because the work involved was more a matter of translating technical jargon into plain or even interesting English than telling near-lies to ill-educated people in order to persuade them to buy things that might be useless or harmful, and that they probably could not afford. I am really lucky at least not to have that kind of thing on my conscience. Anyway, if you added together all the clients I dealt with, they came to a reasonable slice of the agency's revenue.

At the Tavistock I sat once a week in a colourless room with a very interesting group of people, most of them in well-paid jobs, and tried to sort myself out in a co-operative way, and not to get more than my share – though *attention* from an articulate group of people with troubles of their own is not quite like attention from the particular person you want it from as a child. I became calmer and happier over the space of a few months, and finally said goodbye to the group and Dr Malan. By this time they had become friendly on the whole, and easier to be with, though not fun.

Jackie and I went back to Chelsea – we were living in Walpole Street – and eventually moved into a slightly larger flat in my old mews, but at the narrow entrance to the mews instead of at the bottom. Someone at Notley's organized a collection for a wedding present and we spent the money on a vast assortment of things, ranging from an oversize brass bed to a 78 rpm record of Marlene Dietrich singing 'You Go to My Head'. Jackie was doing television shows, particularly a monthly one which went out live from Cardiff on Sundays, called *Land of Song*.

Jackie and I did not enjoy complete and unclouded happiness for more than a few months. She found an old diary of mine, antedating our acquaintance, and was what appeared to me furiously angry. In fact I suppose there was a great deal of anxiety mixed up with it. Over the next few months I dared hardly look at another woman while we were together. It didn't occur to me to conclude hastily that I had made a mistake: in fact I 'knew' I hadn't made a mistake. This was the person. No doubt we both began a long and difficult time waiting for each other to change. She waited for me to become totally faithful, which seemed to me to mean something tame and dull; I waited for her to become less, well, anxious. We went to Corsica the following summer and saw the Marchands and Andrée and Suzanne. By that time I was busy translating all Rimbaud's poetry, including the great prose poems. I had also had a first book of poems accepted by Putnam, whose reader at that time was John Pudney. Before Christmas Jackie was pregnant, and we began to be friendly with the Irish district nurse who had been my neighbour in the mews for a long time. Early in 1961 on a Saturday morning we leant out of the hay-door above the cobbles and asked 'Mrs Mac' – her name was McEvoy – up for a drink. Maybe the traffic in Ladbroke Road drowned what I said, but she looked up at Jackie and said in her nice gruff voice: 'Are ye in labour?'

Joe was born in April 1961 at the Elizabeth Garrett Anderson Hospital off Haverstock Hill. Ironically he's the only one of my children I didn't see born: it was a women-only hospital. I don't think anything changed me or surprised me or took me over quite so much as that event. I think if I'd had time in the next weeks and months I should have been able to realize how happy I was and how much more real I seemed to be. As it was, I had plenty of work at Notley's, but I took long lunch-hours to come and enjoy another chance of seeing the little fellow. I found out about and became very conversant with gripe-water and nappies and crying – and later with tins of baby food, and pram and push-chair navigation. I walked miles, I suppose, round our two rooms, thinking what a good job it was that I'd done so much manual work as to have strong arms, and what a pity my hearing was so good. Later, I became very well acquainted with Paddington Station, and was extremely grateful to the driver who invited Joe up on to the footplate of one of the last steam locomotives to work at Paddington.

Nearly two years later Emma was born in the mews. This was equally marvellous because I was there all the time. At the Elizabeth Garrett Anderson Hospital Jackie had been much upset by the strictness about feeding-times. In fact I had to be aggressively anti-authoritarian in order to drive out all that discipline and get her to do things when she felt like it rather than when she thought she should. Having a baby in your own bed did seem right, and right enough for me to be civil to the district nurse who came – not Mrs McEvoy but a midwife from elsewhere. She seemed to me a bit less aware of people than I expected her to be. Joe was asleep downstairs, Jackie was beyond calling exhausted, and there was Emma, extraordinary, luminously beautiful, and actually a little blue. There was snow outside. Into the cot went Emma, and off went the midwife. Civil to the last, I turned and raced to put on a kettle and fill a very hot-water bottle. I took Emma out and held her while the bottle warmed the cot. When I thought it was hot I took out the bottle and replaced it with Emma. I was very glad to be there.

Katie was born in Norfolk, a couple of miles across fields from where I write this. The house had been a pub, a beerhouse like the Trowel and Hammer, with no bar but a front room with settles and a fireplace, and a beer store at the back where pints would be drawn and then brought in. It is still called the Walnut Tree, and has one growing in front of it, a bit to the side. I planted another one on the other side for when the old one goes.

When Katie was born it was my first term as 'Senior English Master' at Eye Grammar School, thirteen miles away. One hundred and twenty boys and girls, six people in the Upper Sixth English group doing A levels, and a headteacher who seemed rather to represent his staff in his dealings with the education officer than pass on the latter's point of view to the staff. All he seemed to care about when I asked for time off on the Feast of St Cecilia was whether Jackie was all right.

At least Nurse Peeling had a bark and a bite that could be compared to each other – the bark was worse – and was thoroughly awake to everything. She was outspokenly in favour of delivering girl babies rather than boy babies, and perhaps thought she was making up for this startling piece of information when on my arrival with hot water or whatever else she ordered that night and morning she said 'Good boy! Good boy!' as if I'd been Richmal Crompton's William instead of a respectable grammar-school teacher. I buried the afterbirth under the plum tree and came back to have another look at Kate. Nurse Peeling had done well; Jackie had been heroic and beautiful; and there was Katie, utterly sweet. We were all there. Everyone was there. Having a family is no joke: I've observed this and taken some part in the non-joking aspect of it. But it is a sort of miracle, all the more so for being an unsentimental affair.

55

The Tavistock Clinic can't be blamed for failing to turn me into a normal person, whatever that is, or even for not having changed the way I regarded women. At fourteen I was above all interested in getting away from my mother, and my guess is that everything was fine so long as I was what Auden calls 'the more loving one' – a phrase that deserves scrutinizing. What I couldn't take was expressions of love from women, especially if they could possibly be interpreted as in any way proprietorial: *My* dear, *My* lover, *My* man. However, Jackie was and is not just a remarkably attractive person, but a remarkable person, and I was incredibly lucky to find myself agreeing with her about these amazing children at every stage, and quite happily taking part in caring for them as much as I had time for when not working. I was luckier than she in having a variety of jobs, and in being less tied to the one kitchen sink; but I understood very well the leanness of the mother and the exhaustion that is ignored because the children are actually the most important people in the family at the time. We parted because she was – quite reasonably – anxious about what I at first might be, and eventually was, up to with other women; and because I was, irrationally, anxious about belonging to myself and not (even) to her. We both belonged to the children, and still do. I stayed with Jackie ten years beyond the point when I began to feel unhappy staying with her, and when I moved away I moved only to the next village. I never stopped seeing all of them; and not long after Jackie and I parted we became friends. For all this I am grateful; and very grateful to her.

Well yes, and to the children too, who are far from children now. What does it matter, I jokingly ask, if they are brilliant, interesting, intelligent, witty, street-wise or learned? The fact is, they're kind and generous and thoughtful: they're nice people. That's something to be grateful for even a little of, but what I've got is full measure, pressed down and running over. Too much, if one had to deserve it.

56

The principle of payment in inverse proportion to the hardness of the work seems to operate throughout state education, and I was always wryly amused to be told by headteachers and others in schools I worked in for my last seven years in education that we drama advisers were the only ones who seemed actually to *do* anything in schools. 'The others pop in and have a cup of coffee, push a few books at you, tell you the latest gossip, and then say "I must be off, I'm having lunch in King's Lynn at one!"' Norfolk County Council was careful not to call us drama advisers but 'peripatetic area drama teachers', and to pay us as Scale II teachers, even though we spent many of our long hours advising headteachers and heads of drama departments and of English, none of these on less than Scale IV. My friend Gill Doel is a hard-working slide librarian as well as a photographer, and would understand the joke.

When I first knew Gill she was working at the art school in Norwich, and having a little exhibition for which she wrote some notes, quite simple and unassuming ones, from which I learnt a big thing. In them, she observed that energy and love were in some way interchangeable forms of the same thing. This is what made me want to get acquainted with her.

We had one really awful moment though: she got me stopped, driving the car in Norwich one night. By the time I'd got out of Bethel Street Police Station next morning – where a blood test, or rather a urine test, had revealed to everyone's satisfaction that I was not over the legal limit for alcohol – I had been done for 'possession': and for 'growing' too.

After I left Jackie I spent a long time looking for somewhere to live. I needed a place near the Walnut Tree because I couldn't risk making visits difficult for the children or myself, and was determined not to stop seeing them. While this was going on I lived more or less in the car, which was half full of books and clothes and even food. Quite a lot of people put me up, particularly the Barkers, Edward and Ruth, at Newton Flotman. They lent me a little painting studio beyond Edward's sculpture studio, and when it got cold they let me sleep in their daughter's room. She was at college somewhere.

Meanwhile I went on being West Norfolk area drama specialist, and spent four days a week teaching in eight different schools, changed every half-term, in front of the teachers whose classes I taught; and one day a week at County Hall, exchanging ideas and experience with my colleagues, listening to my superiors, and devising evening and vacation courses for serving teachers. Oh, and helping amateur drama groups where possible in the evenings. Ill-paid or not, it was still a marvellous job. We decided which schools to visit, and made our own timetables; we formed our own Theatre in Education team; at one point we even tried to do *commedia dell'arte* outdoors at fêtes and things, which was very brave. Amateur drama societies may be comically riven with conflicting interests and tense with competitiveness: people who work in educational drama are unlikely to be anything but friends with their colleagues, because educational drama is not competitive. Members of drama classes actually have to be able to help each other, and drama teachers have to try to turn 'Form 4G' into a group who get on well together before they can begin to do drama with them.

Not many decades ago it used to be said in Norfolk that a farm-worker needs precious little education (and precious little money either once he is working), but we drama people responded to poor pay and demanding work with a cheerful determination not to be distracted from *our* work by *their* attitudes. Morale in the mid-seventies was still very high.

What happened with Gill and me was that one evening we attended someone else's drama workshop in St Benedict's Street – a much-needed change for me after I had spent weeks running my own classes and workshops, which meant an uninterrupted outflow of energy and ideas with not much coming in. After the class we went for a drink at the Eight Bells, and Gill suddenly remembered she had no lights on her bike. 'Don't worry,' I said. 'I'll drive behind you very slowly, and no one will notice you've got no lights.'

Gill duly set off and turned right at the bottom of Grapes Hill where it said BUSES ONLY. 'Dear dear,' said I to myself, and followed her.

Out popped a police car, and it followed me towards Heigham Street.

'Excuse me, sir, but you've just committed a moving traffic offence. Would you blow into this?'

Along we went to Bethel Street, with another policeman driving my car. The test, after the regulation delay, proved negative; but at some doorway I was met by a bearded hippie, except for the coldness of his eye, waving a small polythene bag in my face: 'Wossis, then?'

I looked at him and at it, swallowed, and said: 'Herbs, I suppose.'

In no time at all I found myself sitting on a desk in a large deserted office upstairs with rows of desks, surrounded – I shan't say menaced – by three or four policemen and a policewoman. They wanted to know where I'd got this polythene bag. By this time I'd remembered: it was a small gift from a friend who also taught in Norfolk, though not in my area. I hadn't had time to smoke any; I'd been too busy. I told them I'd grown it.

Dear old Edwin Brock, my fellow-poet and once my fellow-copywriter, was wonderful as I reached this stage of the story. 'What you *should* have said – *ohhh Oliver!* – what you should have said, was: "I've never, seen it, before, in my life! That's all! I've never seen it before in my life! *I* dunno how it got there! I give people lifts. . . ."'

Soon after this, I was in court. No reporters: it was at the end of the list, in the annexe – which is now a picture gallery. The Revd Anthony Lathe, then the Quidenham group rector, was kind enough to come with me. 'I can't do anything for you in court, but we could have a beer afterwards.'

I was fined £150, which Anthony said was lenient. I thought I should tell my immediate superior, so I did. I felt suddenly very tired and dispirited when he said with perfect rectitude that he'd have to inform the assistant education officer.

I was suspended for several months, until an education employment subcommittee, one of whose members – a local landowner – asked me whether I would encourage my children to smoke cannabis, sacked me by a majority decision.

The National Union of Teachers was very good, and got me an Industrial Tribunal hearing. The judge on the tribunal, a curiously learned man, surprised me by treating Norfolk County Council's representative with some severity, advising him to familiarize himself with certain previous cases, and delivering what was almost a short lecture on the poet Coleridge and his indulgence in laudanum. My immediate superior surprised me too: he gave the tribunal a glowing testimonial on me and my work, as well as referring to the thirty or so letters of support which the County Education people had received from head-teachers at whose schools I had worked. Indeed it was one of them, Chris, at Stoke Ferry, who had told me to stop despairing and go and see . . . he started to give me a list of likely headteachers. He was and probably still is an evangelical Christian.

In a break during the proceedings, to my initial embarrassment and confusion, I almost bumped into the judge. 'Did you mind what I said about Coleridge?' he asked.

'Um, no. No, not at all. In fact I like . . . I admire Coleridge very much,' said I.

'Mind you,' he said, leaning towards me almost confidentially, 'I don't think it was laudanum that harmed him: *I blame German metaphysics.*'

I laughed. I couldn't help loving the old boy. 'Thank you,' I said.

'This man must be given back his job,' he told the not very happy-looking County Council lawyer. 'And don't forget those cases I gave you.'

Norfolk appealed, so there were more weeks of waiting. The appeal was heard in St James's Square, and my daughter Emma came with me. The NUT solicitor was perhaps thirty years old. Norfolk had hired a fairly eminent QC called Mitchell, at I can't guess what fee. We won, anyway. I went back to work after almost a year's break, paid back my unemployment benefit and received my back-pay. I bought a stereo deck, amplifier and loudspeakers, though I didn't have much time to play them, working at my hundred-odd schools and doing courses for teachers and so on.

The sad obscurity I lived in for those months of suspension and unemployment – I hardly began to feel any sort of pinch financially – were lightened by many things. I began to write poems again, and to get them published too. My closest colleague visited me to drink beer and discuss 'this sorry Scheme of Things', as Edward Fitzgerald makes Omar Khayyám call it, and to 'Re-mould it nearer to the Heart's Desire'.

Anthony Lathe found me work to do, searching in the old parish registers for genealogical information for American correspondents, and I was asked to contribute to performances in local churches, by writing or acting or speaking. This made me feel much more like going to church on Sundays. I felt something of this sort: if they supported me in adversity, why shouldn't I support them in theirs? George Barker remarked of an Anglican vicar in Itteringham at this time (about 1980) that he couldn't help feeling sad to think of how few people they had to preach to on Sunday mornings.

I even joined the Parochial Church Council (unaware that I hadn't been baptized) and attended meetings, most of whose time was taken up with fund-raising for the maintenance of church fabric. When I suggested to an incoming vicar that we might spend a quarter of an hour at these meetings discussing something other than money, such as 'the Christian life', he brightened up and agreed. Unfortunately he put it to the vote.

At the same time I was becoming a keen nuclear disarmer. Jackie and I had done a whole Aldermaston march before Joe was born: she had carried a placard most of the way bearing a photograph of Bertrand Russell. After the Trafalgar Square finale to the march, she had vaulted over a Soho pillar-box: a small quantity of beer is a powerful restorative to the healthy and abstemious. In 1982, in February (the day, I later discovered, that my friend Paul Nicholson killed himself by diving off the Menai Bridge on to some rocks), I began a long vigil outside the Erpingham Gate of Norwich Cathedral Close. People were extraordinarily nice, I thought. A waiter from the Maid's Head Hotel would bring me a snack on a tray during the morning. When this failed – perhaps someone complained – the Tatler Restaurant sent me endless cups of coffee. I stood there on most days from about ten in the morning till five in the afternoon, for more than a year.

What made me do it was a remark by the then Bishop of Norwich, an ex-naval man who wore medal ribbons on his stole – the scarf-like thing you have wear when giving the blessing to a congregation. He was reported at that time as saying that he would be willing to *press the button* himself if necessary. I still find this offensive rather than defensive; and apropos of which, shouldn't the MOD really be the MOO? What was wrong with 'the War Office' anyway?

The Bishop of Norwich in February 1982 was the Rt. Revd Maurice Wood. His chaplain was the Revd Bob Drayson. The late Canon James Gilchrist was completely charming – courteous and generous and kind. He was also a bit unpredictable. At Anthony Lathe's fiftieth birthday party there was, among the many and varied guests, a large person I took for an Arab, and thought: What a lot of interesting people Anthony knows! It turned out to be James, who had attired himself thus in order to come and celebrate Anthony's *Abrahamic majority*, he said.

The people going in and out of the cathedral and King Edward School would stop and talk, mostly in a friendly sense. Canon Gilchrist's wife would come and say: 'James says, after you've finished, would you like to come and have some tea?' Even the bishop's chaplain, a charming person called Bob (I forget his surname), would stop and talk very kindly and candidly. The bishop himself would give me a very wide berth on the few occasions I saw him, yelling graciously 'Ahh! Yes! My friend from CND!' but never slackening his pace.

George Barker, whose sons were at the school in the close, not knowing I was there, stopped in his tracks and then walked towards me with open arms and kissed me. George was a great one for the kiss: indeed it is a succinct expression of approval or affection.

Christian CND got to know about this vigil; in fact I probably told them. I'd sold a fair member of their pamphlets, particularly one that contained quotations from various Anglican and Catholic bishops denouncing nuclear weapons. My first placard said: BISHOPS AGAINST THE BOMB. When the pamphlets ran out, I painted another placard which said – my only advertising jingle: THE C of E SHOULD BE NUCLEAR-FREE.

Christian CND Council, which I soon joined, contained a lot of very freely spoken Christians, from Quakers to Catholics (extremes meet on a sphere or planet), and I found I liked them all. We tended to talk less about the Bomb than about the Church: on a pilgrimage to Canterbury I found that both I and the national organizer were thinking about 'going over' or some such euphemism, and we started laughing. I felt very happy.

I was instructed by Fr. Brendon Peters, using at my suggestion the catechism just then published by the Catholic Truth Society, written by the Dominican scholar and teacher Fr. Herbert McCabe, OP. Brendon was dry but clear – 'more like a maths teacher than an English teacher', I told Barbara Eggleston. He baptized me on 22 December 1985 in the church belonging to the Carmelite Monastery at Quidenham, and I was received into the Roman Catholic Church.

James Gilchrist worked for a long time in retirement cataloguing church silver in Norfolk. His surname has an appropriate etymology: it means 'servant of Christ'. He once said that if I was fined again for cutting American fences, he would pay the fine. I told him that he would not be doing me a favour if he did; I'd prefer to go to prison.

'It worries me that you're angry,' he said.

'I'm not angry. Truly. Not with Mrs Thatcher, anyway. I suppose I get a bit angry when I see poor people bullied or ignored.'

At this point he surprised me by saying: 'Well, I get angry.'

'What makes you angry?' I asked, smiling.

'Well . . . this business of women priests.'

'And what aspect of that makes you angry, James?'

'It's all taking far too long!'

When I stopped laughing, he raised a finger and said: 'But I've had a sign – from God.'

'What form did it take?'

'Well, you know, the other day I asked one of the Sisters in Magdalen Street to tea, and she said: "Can I bring a friend?" So I said: "Yes! Bring a friend, if you like." So she came. I stood in the doorway as she came in, and behind her there was this tall black woman. And you know she had something – I noticed something – white, here, round her neck! And I said: "Are you a priest?" And she said: "Yes!" And, you know, we joined hands – and danced round the kitchen table!'

Katie was seventeen at the time I started the cathedral vigil. When she heard that I had to park the car in a free parking place and go and move it every so often, she introduced me to the then dean of the cathedral whose daughter was a friend, and he very kindly let me park in the driveway of his house in the close. The Very Revd David Edwards is now Provost of Southwark Cathedral. Katie always seems to know everyone.

57

Fifty years ago at Central Books I used to find myself packing into book parcels small quantities of *Country Standard*. It now appears in larger format on nice white paper with the title in green, inside a long green banner. Underneath it says: *Founded 1936. . . . For Peace and Socialism in the Countryside. . . . 40p*. It started as a union paper for farm-workers, and you always see it at the September Burston Strike School Rally, outside the school itself, which was built with contributions from all over the world. The stones on its façade bear the names of trade-union branches in the north, in the United States and in Wales. One stone just says LEO TOLSTOY.

I gave *Country Standard* the following article after spending seventeen days in HM Prison, Norwich. They were pleased to print it, but they left out the bit about Harold Robbins.

* * *

I once met a psychology student who told me about rats. The more you crowd them together, apparently, the worse they behave. At some point they start eating each other.

I don't suppose overcrowding in prisons is *really* a Home Office policy intended to solve the population problem, but in any case I'm grateful that in Norwich Prison, where I spent a couple of weeks last month, the management's response to overcrowding has been to try to make it bearable instead of lethal.

What they've done is, quite simply, to relax. Something's got to give, after all.

Instead of barking at you, and insisting on bullshit in the cell and silence in the exercise yard, they occasionally smile, call you 'Pop' if you're over 60, and during the day if a prisoner asks them they actually let him out of his cell for a serious visit to the lavatory.

Anything less serious goes in a plastic bucket which prisoners have to empty twice a day at 'slop-out'. It is important to keep the lid on the bucket as long, and as tight, as possible.

The food is really quite reasonable – occasionally better than you get on some motorways – and there's enough of it. The porridge (what else?) at breakfast time can be good. Perhaps it's a bit under-salted. On Saturdays and Sundays there's corn flakes, and sometimes egg and bacon.

They murder vegetables of course, but what institution doesn't? Anyway there's nearly always a choice of main dish at lunch and tea, and there's always plenty of bread. I think this is an important way of keeping people contented.

Another way is physical comfort. Personally, I can't stand anything but cotton touching my skin. Prison underwear and overalls, jeans and T-shirts, and blue twill jackets, are all cotton, and you can change them once a week for clean ones. As for keeping myself clean, I could have showered twice a day every day if I'd looked sharp about it.

Exercise is taken anticlockwise in a big yard for about 40 minutes at a time – long enough to walk a couple of miles if you feel like it – or to watch other people do so if you don't.

There are three films a week: videos on a small screen in a daylit hall. Most films seem to be about war or crime. After seeing two or three I used the opportunity to stay in the cell by myself –

without Radio 2 blasting away, and without a card game going on – just to enjoy a bit of peace.

Peace was what I was in there for. Some of my mail actually said so: 'Oliver Bernard, Peace Prisoner,' it was addressed. I had refused to pay fines of £300-odd incurred by cutting or attempting to cut fences at air bases, as part of the Snowball Campaign. This was started in Norfolk in 1983 by three women. It has since spread to all parts of Britain, and thousands of people have done one or more cuts. Snowball campaigners say that the campaign will stop as soon as Britain starts voting consistently for multilateral disarmament in the United Nations, *or* officially endorses the Freeze Campaign, *or* takes some independent step towards getting rid of our own nuclear weapons.

Obviously making us pay fines is a nice quiet way of dealing with it. That's why many of us prefer prison. It makes for conversation in your local village or community. People begin to think you really mean what you say.

And that's why I didn't mind being in prison – even if it had been a much nastier place. Unlike my seven cell-mates – in a room about twelve by eighteen feet – I was where I wanted to be.

But if I was the most fortunate person in the main block of Her Majesty's Prison, Norwich, I was on top of a pretty tall heap. What I discovered, in this ice-cream-coloured Victorian bird-cage, with a cast-iron staircase rising three tiers above ground level in the middle of it, was that there aren't really degrees of wickedness so much as degrees of misfortune. I couldn't honestly pretend that I or anyone was *incapable* of committing anything anyone else was in for. I just saw that I was pretty well off, and that others were less so.

I don't envy the screws their jobs, though I admired the patience and decency of some of them. Six of my cell-mates, I believed, ought to have been doing community service. The seventh, most of us agreed, should have been being looked after in a mental hospital or sheltered accommodation. I can't say much about other, longer-term, prisoners, because I don't know much. Murder and manslaughter and armed robbery and fraud don't set the people who do them so very far apart from other sinners. But I'm certainly no expert on crime and punishment.

I found a quite impressive sort of tact and consideration among prisoners though. People really made great efforts not to tread on each other's toes. I never saw anyone collide with anyone else, and I never heard anyone ask anyone else what they were in for. It just wasn't done.

But it *was* a social heap: and at the bottom of it, as in other prisons, were the Rule 43 men. Rule 43 means that for their own protection certain prisoners are segregated at all times – for food, exercise, slop-out etc. – from other prisoners. They are a mixture of informers, sexual offenders and others, and they are regarded as absolutely beyond the pale. They really do need to be protected from the rest of the prisoners. People literally spit in their food or on their heads, given half a chance. They supply the seemingly necessary class of people who are 'even worse than us'.

I found attitudes to 'nonces' rather unconvincing. (NONCE: (2) A sexual deviant or pervert, esp. one that assaults children – Partridge: *A Dictionary of Slang and Unconventional English.*) First, I couldn't believe that they were subhuman, even if they'd done horrible things. Second, the generalisation was wildly unjust. Fancy spitting or dropping a dog-end in the tea of a bloke who's helped uncover some Mafia operation, in the mistaken belief that he's a child-molester! It's not on.

Dog ends, you can imagine, are smaller and thinner inside than anywhere 'on the out'. Tobacco really is *the* important thing. So important, I already knew, that I took in a really big tin, – and then stopped smoking all the time I was inside. So I was able to give it away on thin days, and to be independent. I spent my £1.40 a week on letters, instead of a meagre $\frac{3}{4}$oz of tobacco, which would just have kept me obsessed with smoking and the craving to smoke.

What got me, in the end, was Radio 2. I must admit I gave up most of my heavy reading for the last three or four days, and read pulp fiction or joined in the card games. It was the line of least resistance. My concentration was shot.

One bit of pulp fiction gave me a certain amount of amusement. I was quietly zipping through a junk-novel by the rich and famous Harold Robbins when I came across a real schoolboy howler: 'He groaned in a strange combination of pleasure and pain as his almost empty testicles strained to express the semen. . . .'

'Good Lord!' I said to the bloke who'd lent me the book.

'Harold blooming Robbins *doesn't know the facts of life*!'

'Hmm. That's a bit beyond me,' he said.

As a Catholic – and quite a recent convert – I was for some reason rather cheered to see that I had a red cell-card, Anglicans etc. having white ones. I found that Mass was celebrated in the prison chapel on Mondays. Only about eight convicted prisoners, and about half-a-dozen men on remand, attended on the two Mondays I went: I missed Mass on the Monday I came into prison because I was in court most of the day in Diss.

The priest who celebrated seemed to have very little to do with the management. He had a big smile and brought two sisters (parish workers) – one of whom I recognised – with him. I waited eagerly for his sermon and was not disappointed. There was absolutely no suggestion that we were a race apart – 'criminals' – though there was the feeling that we were all in trouble. But he made it clear that he had his own experience of trouble too, even if it didn't involve the law.

Afterwards, to my amazement, we all stood about for ten or fifteen minutes chatting and smiling, even laughing (instead of being shooed back to our cells). Father Rogers turned out to know several friends in the peace movement. To cap it all, a long-serving prisoner handed each of us a white cup and saucer containing instant coffee – the only drink except for weak tea that I ever saw in prison. 'Real instant coffee!' I told them, back in the cell.

'Cor! *You're* all right then, Pop.'

On my last morning I was woken at six to get my bed-roll and belongings together, ready to be out of the gate by seven. I followed the tradition of taking a jug, not a mug, down the iron staircase, grabbed my bacon sarny, and carried the jug up again.

'Got some tea there, have you?' said a straight-faced screw. 'Yes thank you,' I said, and reached the empty staircase. I'd never seen it empty before – and I'd never, all the time I was there, been jostled on it, or seen a tray or a mug spilt on it.

My cell-mates enjoyed their sip of early morning tea. They wouldn't be unlocked till I'd walked to the other side of Norwich with my books, my empty tobacco-tin, and all those letters people had written me.

I had a second breakfast with my friend Howard Cresswell, Vicar of St. Barnabas, who started Norwich Christian CND in 1982.

It was one of those sunny, chilly mornings. . . . I must say I felt grateful to just about everyone.

58

Getting into Norwich Prison was more difficult than getting into the Central School of Speech and Drama in 1970. For the latter I did, it's true, have to audition for a whole day; but for Norwich I had to 'commit criminal damage' more than a dozen times by cutting a strand of chain-link fencing at Sculthorpe, Watton, Coltishall, Corsham, Burghfield and Upper Heyford, and to travel to court about twenty-five times to be fined, or to refuse to pay fines. This does not include drawing crosses and writing on the Portland stone walls of the Ministry of Defence on various Ash Wednesdays, and the consequent court appearances in London during Lent.

In all these activities except the incident at Watton I was with friends from my village or surrounding ones, or from farther afield in the case of Christian actions. The Snowball campaign was started by Angie Zelter in north Norfolk, and spread as far as Cornwall, Wales and Scotland. The first person to go to prison in my village was a lady of fairly advanced years, a vicar's widow, who came back from Holloway saying that 'the Staff were very good', as if it had been some sort of hotel. After the first time, when four or five of us travelled to Sculthorpe in a minibus from Snetterton feeling both nervous and excited after a shared breakfast, it became just a bit exciting, and cheerful. People probably get the same feeling when fox-hunting. But no blood; not even opposition. We were after all very keen on co-operating with the police, who wanted us in court. On more than one occasion I've had to go to police stations and denounce myself, so to speak. This was the case when Angie and I spent at least ten minutes first cutting and then unravelling the chain-link, plastic-coated wire on the main gates of RAF Coltishall, and were asked by the guard who we were working for. When we said 'The Snowball Campaign' the guard said 'Oh'. Half-way back to the gatehouse he broke into a run: it was a sort of walking double-take. We had to go to North Walsham Police Station. When they asked us what we wanted, Angie said: 'We've come to report a crime.'

Another time, on my sixth or seventh cut, not being able to get anyone to do it with me that afternoon (this was at RAF Watton), I did it alone. I went to Watton Police Station and warned them politely that I was going to cut the fence up the road in about a quarter of an hour, and the man on duty asked me to please make it about thirty-five minutes because it was so near the end of the shift and the wives would have got the tea ready.

Unfortunately the magistrates found, or were shown, a rather cunning way of getting round refusals to pay: it is now permitted to withhold money from teachers' pensions at source. So I may never qualify for another term of prison.

I ought, though, to have said something about the Central School of Speech and Drama. I had a very intensive year there during which I became qualified, on paper at least, to teach educational drama in schools, and thus got into my last and best period of full-time employment. But I learnt a great deal besides: how to relax physically, and in some degree how to perform. I became acquainted with Interaction at Oval House, and with the amazing Trêtaux Libres company which was visiting London in 1970–1, and finally with Theatre Machine. I went to Central thinking I had some notion of speaking verse, but I had my horizons enormously expanded there, so that now I can make reasonable tapes of prose books for the blind, perform my own Rimbaud translations by heart to a live audience, and even read my brother Jeffrey's *Spectator* columns on Radio 4. For this I feel particularly grateful to Gerard Benson, to John Roberts and to Sue Lefton – wherever they may be. And to the Central School, which I need not commend as a very distinguished institution.

As for poetry, I haven't insisted too much on the verse I've written; or quoted from it. Writing this account or confession has kept me busy enough not to feel bad about how little poetry I actually produce, or to worry about its quality. Presumably now it's done, the general uncomfortableness of being a verse-writer will return. That is nothing to complain about, though.

Afterword

I don't know about clouds of glory. When anybody asks me what was the happiest moment in my life I don't know the answer. Probably there is no knowing, since happiness is a much less conscious state of being than its opposite. Lately I have been thinking of a plank bridge I'm crossing, wearing sandals and faded blue shorts. It's July 1932 at Old Hurst, Milford, and I'm about seven. I may never go to school again. The house smells of oak smoke and beeswax, and a stream runs at the bottom of the garden. Cows come and drink from it on the other side, and beneath a bridge under the road you can see a far stretch of green, a meadow where I've seen carthorses rolling on their backs for pleasure. Where I'm going this morning is to find the source of the stream, its highest point. I want to see this utter purity bubbling out of the stones somewhere, before anything can live in it, or muddy it, or bridge it; the place where no one even drinks from it because they haven't found it.